Endorsements

"An invaluable resource for the author struggling with the elusive art of promotion. Highly recommended!"
--Wendy Howell Mills, Author of Outer Banks mystery series and *Island Intrigue,* first of a new series

"Whether you have a major publishing house behind your book or you are self- published, the reality is: If the books get promoted and sold, you are going to have to be the one to do it. *Published! Now Sell It!,* the collaborative effort of five published authors, is well-written, well-organized, and contains an abundance of marketing ideas for those who are seriously interested in taking control and giving their book a chance to succeed in today's highly-competitive book market. If you want your book to be a financial success, you will not want to miss the many opportunities to market your book that are presented here by the authors who have used them."
--Richard V. Bailey
Publisher Critics' Choice

"What a great idea! *Published! Now Sell It!* is filled with personal experiences showing the reader the in's and out's of 'right on' book promotion."
—Rick Frishman, President of Planned TV Arts, Co-author, *Guerrilla Marketing for Writers and Guerrilla Publicity*

"Whether you sell out to a large New York publisher or publish yourself, the author must do the promotion. Publishers do not promote books. This insightful book is full of down-to-earth advice from authors who know from experience how to promote and sell books. Learn what these authors wish they had known when they first published their books. From niche marketing to media interviews—take an inside look at marketing and publicity from the viewpoint of experienced authors."

—Dan Poynter, *The Self-Publishing Manual*

"*Published! Now Sell It!* is full of practical tips and real-life stories. If the authors follow their own advice, this book should reach plenty of readers and writers."

—Paul Aron, Author, *50 Day Trips From Williamsburg*

"Many a book from a novice author collects dust in a book warehouse, because they assume the publisher will take care of their book's promotion. WRONG. For a book to be a success, the author needs to be dedicated to getting the book in the public literary buzz. *Published! Now Sell It!* offers a guide to set up a promotional book campaign from five authors who have been there."

Joyce Dixon
Southern Scribe

Best Wishes
Jean C. Keating

PUBLISHED!
NOW SELL IT!

A "how to" book
with focus on promotion
For Authors
By Authors

A primer for writers with books to sell, written by authors
with experience in promotion, publicity, and selling
in today's expanding marketplace

Edited by Mary Montague Sikes and Olen Sikes

Contributing Authors

Joseph Guion
E. R. Kallus
Jean C. Keating
Mildred H. B. Roberson
Mary Montague Sikes

BookWaves

PUBLISHED! NOW SELL IT!
A "How To" Book
with focus on promotion

Published by:
BookWaves, LLC
P.O. Box 182
West Point, VA

The authors and publisher have provided information herein on their personal experiences with selling and promoting their books. They assume no responsibility or liability for specific applications by any individual or group with their own publishing and marketing ventures. Readers should consult an attorney or accountant for professional advice where applicable.

First Edition, December 2005

Cover Design, Mary Montague Sikes

Library of Congress Cataloging-In-Publication Data

Library of Congress Control Number: 2005928368

ISBN: 0-9769832-0-6

A "How To" Book with focus on promotion by authors for authors

1. Authorship—Marketing 2. Books—Marketing 1. Title

10 9 8 7 6 5 4 3 2 1

Acknowledgements

Published! Now Sell It! resulted from the combined work of five authors who met over a period of one year discussing and creating the chapters that make up this work. We have included examples of marketing tools and techniques we found most helpful in marketing our own published work. We also point out other sources that have proved useful to us as writers.

Many people have made this work possible. We are especially grateful to Paul Aron who met with us and helped inspire our writing for this book. George Coussoulos met with us for several months and aided in the process of developing *Published! Now Sell It!* We have enjoyed conversations with Joe Sabah and have found inspiration in his weekly newsletter. Sylvia Wright and Ginger Levit shared their expertise for our chapter on television appearances. Carl and Jenny Loveland were kind to provide us with a wealth of knowledge about building websites. Additional information has come from publications of the Federal Government, public libraries, personal contacts, and a variety of websites.

Our thanks go to the staff of the main branch of the Gloucester Library where we developed many of the ideas for *Published! Now Sell It!* We enjoyed numerous luncheon meetings at Dolphin Cove Restaurant where we used their large conference room to plan our projects. We thank the staff there.

Thanks also to the many members of the Chesapeake Bay Writers Club who offered their help and support. We appreciate the backing of our family members who have endured the process and evolution of *Published! Now Sell It!*

Table of Contents

CHAPTER ONE

The Honest Truth

by Jean C. Keating

You're a published author! You've just seen your words in print for the first, or maybe more than the first time. The thrill, the pride, the satisfaction is enormous! All those hours and months of writing, editing, restructuring, and planning have finally paid off. Your book or books are a reality.

The last thing you want to hear is that you've finished the easy part and now the real work lies ahead! But this, unfortunately, is the plain and simple truth.

Whether you "won the literary lottery," acquired an agent and an established publisher to publish your work, or went the route of self-publishing or print-on-demand to produce your work, the hardest part of being an author is still ahead: selling the books!

Unless you're a former president or first lady, a high-profile criminal, or an unfortunate celebrity who has made a splash on the major news networks, even the larger publishing houses are not going to provide publicity for your works. If the books get promoted and sold, you are going to have to be the one to do it. Major publishing houses will include your new title in their list of releases, charging back to you a fee for doing so. Even then, you need to understand some simple numbers in order to appreciate how very little of an impression inclusion in such a listing will make on bookstores and buyers.

To understand the challenges a published author faces, you need only consider the numerics of the marketplace. Last year 175,000 *new* books were released: that translates to about twenty per hour! It doesn't take a rocket scientist to figure out that your book is going to be one of many in a long list of new releases. If your book is going to be a success and you are going to be a writer for whom the publisher will consider a second and a third manuscript, you are going to have to do the work of marketing and promoting the printed books. Who else believes in your book as fervently as you do, anyway?

At a recent presentation to a regional literary group, a romance writer working on her fourteenth book was asked by a member of the audience to describe the amount of marketing and publicity help that her publisher, Harlequin

Romances, provided to her after her eight-year relationship with them. Her answer? Very, very little. The publishers put a small line in their monthly magazine that a new book was being released. Otherwise, they did nothing to advertise the release. And she was charged for this at a heady rate for publicity.

This lack of marketing support was shocking to some, but echoed by many in the audience with similar histories and experiences. This veteran writer with thirteen published books to her credit makes the arrangements for ads in romance magazines herself and pays for them herself. She arranges book signings and handles all details and sales. She promotes her books with word of mouth, handouts of bookmarks at conferences and bookstores. She maintains her own website, and much more.

In the chapters that follow, a group of writers shares with you the dos and don'ts of marketing books that worked for them. Read and consider how to put these ideas to work for making your published book a sales success.

"Art is long and time is fleeting."

William Wordsworth Longfellow, *A Psalm of Life*

CHAPTER TWO

How It Came to Be

by E.R. Kallus

A group of writers agreed to collaborate in taking control of our writing careers, elevating our literary station from anonymous scribblers to that of successful, recognized authors, where success means being paid for writing. After a series of meetings, we found ourselves on a figurative pilgrimage, negotiating the dim forests and fog-shrouded fens of the literary world standing between us and our common goal. Like Chaucer's pilgrims who eased the burdens of their journey to Canterbury by sharing stories, we derived sustenance and motivation from sharing experiences and ideas. Each meeting contributed to a growing pool of knowledge we hadn't been able to locate on the bookshelves, and we faced the realization that the only magic in the process of becoming successful comes from a writer's ideas. The rest comes as the result of work.

This little book is a compilation of our thoughts and experience—call it the facts beyond the manuscript. We offer it as a tool we hope you will find very useful in furthering your writing career. As it is with all tools, using the advice presented in its pages first requires decisions and then your commitment to making yourself and your books marketable.

How many writers think of themselves as publishers and salesmen before they begin writing? Precious few. If anything, writers are far more likely to consider themselves solitary geniuses or introspective artists than representatives of their own product. They like to talk about books and enjoy the company of other bookish people, but selling? "Not for me," they'll say in an act of blind faith in a process they know little about.

Literary lore—it's a beguiling thing—describes a heady chain of events beginning with an agent who accepts your book and presents it to a publisher whose presses and publicists do their magic. Your book appears in bookstores, stacked high for avid readers to snap up. You, with your book under consideration as the basis for a movie and your fertile mind freed to do exotic research for another book, hire a new accountant, and depart for a remote island in the Mediterranean with laptop and satellite telephone. Your recently enriched and grateful agent waits for the cycle to begin again with your next manuscript.

Yes, it can happen, to a fortunate few—very, very few. In a real world, it's not that way. Even the best-selling authors work hard and constantly in keeping themselves in the public eye by publicizing themselves, their fellow authors, and their art. Depending on their talents and means, how they do it can include speaking, signing books, being interviewed, maintaining a website, and doing everything they can to create a broader interest in buying books.

A successful book is one that's packaged with its author and marketed well. This means simply that to succeed, authors cannot be satisfied merely to sit at the keyboard conducting the imaginative impulses from their brains to paper. Every author must become an active participant in marketing his or her book.

If you've read this far, it's highly likely that you've already poured your energies and emotions into writing a book. It may already be published or perhaps it's still a manuscript lying on your desk, a three-inch stack of neatly typed pages. Whatever its present form, it's tangible evidence of your genius and work ethic. Just having the kind of persistence and determined dedication to sit in solitary labor pounding out the millions of keystrokes it takes to write a book sets you apart as a special sort of person. It's a proud thing to be able to say that you have a book, but without acclaim and sales the sense of accomplishment fades quickly.

So what about your book? If it's still a manuscript, how will it be published? If it has already been published, how will you market it? Those are questions each of us struggled with alone before we began our pilgrimage together.

The whole point of this book is to tell you that you do indeed have a choice. You can take the path described in literary lore, the old way, and spend many months, even years, in a low-percentage effort that consumes as much time and effort as writing the manuscript in the first place, or take the new way in which you seize control of the process. You decide that your book deserves publication. You have it published and you sell it.

What we mean by the old way is the one with the writer-agent-publisher axis at its core, the standard way, the industry controlled by the major publishing houses. It's large and powerful because it controls a substantial amount of the money generated by selling books—but the industry relies heavily on the slim spectrum of best-selling books to produce its profits. The industry, the few large, big-name companies, is fast evolving into the sole, ever-narrowing market where an author's manuscript is handled from start to finish: publishing, advertising, and placement in bookstores.

The possibility of being relieved of the burden of marketing a book by a big publisher can be an immense attraction to an author who may not yet realize that these publishers are not in business to subsidize new authors. They buy and promote books similar to the ones that have been making money for them. If you haven't noticed yet, there are two big catches in pursuing the old way. First, this system is not likely to publish a first-time author, unless the author already has fame or notoriety. Next is that even authors of bestsellers work actively to sell their books.

The how-to-succeed books avoid giving you the full picture about your responsibility for selling your book. They let you find out on your own, or by reading this book, that the world of publishers and bookstores resembles a capsule enclosing a rarified atmosphere, and that it's almost impossible to enter it.

Partially, it's a matter of numbers. We computer-equipped writers generate a deluge of manuscripts, creating such a surplus of material that the publishers cannot profitably print more than the few that fit their narrow model of a book that they are willing to back with their precious publicity dollars.

Don't misunderstand. Some writers do succeed in getting their works selected, enough so that fortunes are made in publishing books that show writers with new manuscripts supposedly sure-fire ways to interest an agent into representing them, and how to craft a new novel. However, the how-to books don't venture beyond sharing their secrets on writing to match the publishers' models. Wisely, not much effort is made in offering advice on negotiating a contract because so few authors reach that point.

Finding an agent is getting harder, not easier. To continue thinking of the publishing business in terms of numbers, your likelihood of finding an agent by querying and mailing manuscripts is about two percent. The number comes from the agents' own assertions that they reject more than 98 percent of the submissions they get. A two-percent acceptance rate! And that doesn't mean that they sell all they accept. It's slightly better than the lottery, but not as good as putting your money on black or red at the roulette table, yet this narrow avenue to success is touted as the industry standard.

The simple fact is that this "classic" process is enormously expensive in terms of time and energy—far more so than the excruciating labor of writing the book in the first place. And, as every successful author has learned, you still have to sell the book.

You've come to a decision point. It's tempting to spend far too much time in attempting to force the standard wisdom to work because it's the one described in the how-to literature. Or perhaps you fear the unknown of marketing your book yourself. Ask yourself, "Do I make a career of seeking an agent?" Or do I look past the manuscript to see if there's another way?

These are questions that have forced us all to think. You must realize that no matter who pays to have your book printed and bound—you or a publishing house—it is you, the author, who must shoulder the burden for getting it sold. Bella Stander, a literary public relations professional, speaking to the James River Writers Festival in Richmond, underlined that point in discussing promoting novels and non-fiction works as well. She said, "After good writing, to succeed, the author needs to come to one major conclusion. Good writing is an art, but once you have a book it's a product. Get over it. I've met too many authors who don't have a clue about publicity for their books."

That brings you, pilgrim, to taking your most critical look at the old way where the scope of the literary materials published by the big houses is shrinking. In order to survive, the publishing companies are steadily becoming larger individually, while their numbers become fewer.

We pilgrim writers think there's a world of new opportunity expanding, and we want to invite you to join us. That's why we've written *Published! Now Sell It!* We dare to say that readers are demanding a broader variety of books than what is now available. We say the times are changing, and the engines driving the change are an exploding variety of small traditional presses and an even greater expansion of alternative publishers specializing in print-on-demand production. You know from reading the preceding chapter that many thousands of books are published annually, and many thousands more are unnecessarily going unprinted and unappreciated because tax laws and economics make it less attractive for the publishing industry to take chances on new authors. That backlog represents a pent-up pressure already being measured for exploitation. Look, for example, at how major bookstore chains are investing in alternative publishing and creating incentives for striving authors.

We see what's happening in publishing as similar to the enormous changes that occurred in the sale of air travel tickets. Where travel agents once ruled supreme, catered to by airlines, Americans routinely find their best travel deals on the Internet. Similarly, American readers are looking more and more to find new books published and sold by the authors themselves, just as they were in the days before the monolithic publishing industry existed.

In succeeding chapters, you will read of alternative publishing, niche markets, and developing your own publicity program. *Published! Now Sell It!* gives you suggestions and instructions for reaching your goal. Think of each chapter as a stepping stone to making you more capable in representing your work.

Whatever course we followed in making our decisions, the writers whose collaboration produced this book have concluded that struggling in anonymity wasn't enough to meet our goals of recognition and compensation. We writer-pilgrims who contributed our knowledge and experience invite you to take up your pen (or word processor) and join us in self-marketing.

CHAPTER THREE

Niche Marketing: Know How to Target Your Book

by Mildred H. B. Roberson

Niche marketing, by definition, is intended for limited appeal and specialized audiences. However, whether your book explains fly-fishing, offers enchanting poetry for lovers, or is an almanac for organic gardeners, there are several important steps to take when planning the marketing of your book. The following steps are basic to the process and are designed to provide the best return for the money you invest in marketing.

Steps in Niche Marketing

Step One   Identify the possible market(s) for your book.
Step Two   Determine how to find and reach each market.
Step Three Develop a press release applicable for each contact.
Step Four   Contact each market you have identified.
Step Five   Follow up as necessary.

Now let's take a closer look at what is involved in each step.

Step One: Identifying the Market

There are various ways to consider the possible people and places where you may find interest in your book. Three major areas to consider are:

- niches related to the *topic* of your book,
- niches related to the *places or locations* in which your book might be of interest,
- niches related to you, the *author*.

The Topic

First, you need to consider what topic(s) your book addresses. Following are some examples from authors' experiences: The Smith/Roberson book, *My Bag Was Always Packed: The Life and Times of a Virginia Midwife* is the story of a Virginia midwife who was born in 1918 and who practiced from 1950 to 1981. At first glance one might think the book's topic would be limited to childbirth or perhaps midwifery. However, a more expansive view might include women's issues, aspects of African American history, and rural health.

The George Coussoulos book, *Behind Closed Doors: Every Teacher's Chance to Change the World*, focuses on what goes on behind the closed doors of school classrooms and provides insights into the many questions that dedicated teachers should consider. The primary topic is the real role of educators in contemporary schools. But secondary topics involve politics in education, colleges of education, alternative education, and the role of social studies in American education.

A third example of the topic of a book can be seen by looking at Keating's book, *Amorous Accident*. Her book fits into the category of dog stories, but it also would fit into the topic area of mysteries.

The Place or Location

A second major area to consider is niches related to the place or location in which your book might be of interest. Is your book of local, regional, national, or international interest? Even a book that may seem limited to local interest only may have broader appeal. One potential publisher told Roberson that he saw the book as only having appeal to regional markets. Yet some national markets were found to be interested in the topic. For example, The International Center for Traditional Childbearing (ICTC) based in Oregon turned out to be interested enough in the topic to buy 50 copies.

One unique example of a niche related to place is shown by Sikes' book about 20 exceptional hotels and the area sights and scenes close by. The target for the marketing of her book became the 20 cities in which these special hotels are located. Additionally, travelers who might visit the hotels or their environs would also find her book appealing.

The Author

A third niche for you to consider is markets related to you personally. In this category you can consider friends, family, neighbors, and co-workers. One neighbor of Roberson, for instance, liked the book so well that he ordered three more as gifts for others. Another unexpected opportunity arose because Roberson's hairdresser suggested leaving a couple of books in her shop. She has sold seven copies there to date. However, the biggest personal market for the Smith/Roberson book has been the personal connections of Mrs. Smith. Not only her large family and many friends, but clients who were delivered by her during her 30 years of midwifery practice have been buying the book (over 400 so far).

Step Two: Finding and Reaching the Market

Now that you have identified the niches or markets into which your book(s) fit, you are ready to determine how to find and reach each of these markets.

One good place to start is with your local and regional newspapers. If you live, as I do, in a rural area, there may be a number of local papers as well as urban papers that are bought by local residents. Make a list of all your area newspapers with the phone numbers and e-mail addresses for contacting them. Newspapers with large circulations may have a book reviewer on staff. Most papers that I contacted were willing to include a review or press release of my book. (For more information on ways to combine press coverage with book signings please refer to Chapter 5, Conducting Successful Book Signings.)

Another place to search for possible markets for your book(s) is the Internet. There may be many organizations devoted to your topics or sharing your interests. For example, Coussoulos began by finding a site that listed all of the colleges and universities in Virginia so that he could determine the addresses for schools of education.

A third possible contact for you to consider is conferences related to your topics. Writers' conferences held in your area or region may provide an opportunity for you to do a book signing or participate in their program as a presenter. Roberson had an unexpected opportunity to meet the Executive Director of the Virginia Rural Health Association, who then invited her to attend the annual meeting and sell the Smith/Roberson book there.

A fourth possible opportunity to market your book may be found in book reviews appearing in newsletters or journals. (For more information on book reviews, please turn to Chapter 14, Getting Book Reviews.)

A fifth possible market may be identified through speaking engagements or workshops. These topics are discussed in Chapter 7, Utilizing the Radio and Other Public Speaking Events. and Chapter 9, Conducting Workshops.

Lastly, be sure to consider bookstores or other places that sell books. Many stores, especially large ones, prefer to order from a major distributor such as Ingram's, but there may be specialty stores related to your topic. Try them. I found that local bookstores, those within a 50-mile radius, are willing to feature local authors. For example, I discovered that a regional museum sells books by local authors or those writing about regional history. Likewise, a local pharmacy that sells books gives local authors a prominent display location.

Some authors have had success with a smaller distributor, New Leaf Distributing Company. This organization is a wholesaler of books, recorded media, and other products related to spirituality, holistic health, metaphysics, and conscious living. Visit their website to consider whether your book might fit with their interest areas. Please check the appendix for New Leaf contact information.

Step Three: Providing Information to Contacts

You need to be ready to provide a press release. (For more information on writing press releases, please refer to Chapter 4, Marketing with Visuals—Brochures, Press Kits, and More.) I found that some newspapers wanted me to provide the press release and printed it exactly as given. Others edited it, some incorrectly. One editor interviewed me on the phone and wrote her own commentary. An urban paper preferred to go to the book description on the publisher's website, as well as to interview the author by phone.

You also need to be prepared to donate a copy of your book for a review to be written by persons designated by a journal or newsletter. Friends can be helpful. The editor of *The Journal of Multicultural Nursing and Health* asked me to send her a book so that she could ask someone from the editorial board to write a review for the journal.

Step Four: Contact Each Market Identified

Contacts may be made by phone, mail, or in person depending on the circumstances. In rural areas where things are often informal, it seemed best to call newspaper editors to find out if they preferred a written press release, if they wanted a staff member contacted instead, if they preferred an e-mailed contribution, or if they had other requirements. For an urban newspaper there was a book review editor who was both delightful and very helpful!

Coussoulos used his list of university addresses from the Internet as a basis for a letter that was sent to each school of education in Virginia. The letter included a synopsis of his book and his biographical information. College students in these schools are his ultimate niche market. In a similar fashion, after finding the website for ICTC, I contacted the site and established an ongoing communication with its director, herself a licensed African American midwife.

For conferences related to your book topic, you may be able to call or e-mail the conference organizers to see if they allow book signings. The ones in which we have participated were free. When you are a member of an organization that holds annual meetings, it may be especially easy to sell your book at the event.

Always be on the lookout for opportunities to market your book. For example, Coussoulos noticed that his daily newspaper printed a list of "teacher of the year" selections and the schools where each taught. He prepared a letter to send to them suggesting that as outstanding teachers they might be interested in purchasing a book they could share with others in their mutual quest to make significant changes in education.

Step Five: Follow Up as Necessary

Be persistent in contacting people who have expressed an interest in your book but have not yet acted on that interest. They may have intended to follow through and forgot or have gotten sidetracked.

It's also wise to follow up with places that have bought your book or have agreed to sell your book or both. I have found that staff members in stores or museums don't always remember to call me for replacements after all the books that I have provided to them have been sold. You will find variety in arrangements for selling your book. Some places will pay you up front, while others will only pay you after they have sold your book. See Chapter 15 for suggestions on appropriate business practices, record keeping, tax requirements, and related concerns.

Final Tips for Niche Marketing

1. Believe in your book. You wrote it to share your ideas with others.
2. Be creative. Don't limit yourself to the obvious markets for selling your book.
3. Stay alert for unexpected opportunities, such as those mentioned in this chapter and others.
4. Don't get discouraged. Some niche markets that seem logical to you will not show the interest you expected, but others you didn't expect to be helpful will be.

"The bitter and the sweet come from the outside, the hard from within, from one's own efforts."

Albert Einstein, *Out of My Later Years*

CHAPTER FOUR

Marketing with Visuals Brochures, Press Kits, and More

by Mary Montague Sikes

Is a picture worth a thousand words? If so, a quality brochure with good color photographs is a vital tool for both authors and artists to have for book or art promotion. With the newest technology and home office printing equipment, production of a quality product can be simple and rewarding.

This chapter contains information for making brochures, flyers, press releases, and media kits. I used Microsoft Publisher and Adobe PhotoShop Elements in creating my promotional materials.

When choosing fonts for your advertising brochure, you need to take time to check each one out for clarity. If you use too many different styles, your brochure may prove difficult to read and will thus be less effective. Fancy fonts also tend to make the text less legible.

As you work, remember marketing and promoting your writing is no time to be modest. Use your brochures and other marketing materials to point out those things that make your work stand out above the competition and show that you as the creator are special.

Using Microsoft Publisher to Create a Brochure

If you have a computer and software such as Microsoft Publisher, then you are set to produce your own brochure.

To promote my coffee table book, *Hotels to Remember*, I decided to produce a brochure. (See figures 1 and 2 at the end of this chapter.) To create a similar brochure you may follow these instructions.

Open the Publisher program and select the option for brochures. Choose the three-panel option, hit insert on the program bar, then picture from a file.

For my brochure I went to My Images, where photographs of my artwork and books are stored. (You may want to use My Pictures or another folder to store your artwork.) In My

Images I selected a photograph of the cover of *Hotels to Remember* and placed it in the third panel which would become the cover for my brochure. Then I selected the insert text box and typed *HOTELS TO REMEMBER* in capital letters, using the Lucinda Calligraphy font that was selected by my publisher for use on the book cover. Since my book has won contest awards, I added the words, "Award-winning coffee table book" in the same text box beneath the title. Most authors agree it is a good idea to show that your work has been well received by contest judges and by book reviewers.

Now go to the middle panel and decide what you wish to place there. I used the My Images file again and selected two pastel paintings of hotels from *Hotels to Remember* that are also available as giclee signed and numbered fine art prints. That panel forms the back of the brochure.

On the far left panel you may choose to insert a photograph of yourself by using the insert tab from the top bar. After adding a picture on my brochure, I created a text box below the picture and added contact information including e-mail address and website. Another text box located above the photograph is a good place to provide additional information such as "award-winning author and artist."

On the reverse side of the brochure, there is plenty of space for more photographs. On my brochure I inserted three more artwork photographs from the My Images folder and then added information text boxes beneath each picture. Room was left on the middle panel for review comments about the book. The third back panel is a good place for an order form if you wish to include it. My brochure has an order form with prices for my books as well as for my giclee prints from *Hotels to Remember.*

The Publisher program has an option to include a Wizard order form. I did not use it, choosing instead to create an order form of my own.

Another option in Publisher is to include a customer address space on the middle panel. That may be a good idea if you plan to mail out your brochures to potential book buyers. However, my brochures are part of my media kit and also are used for handouts at various meetings and writers' functions, making the address space unnecessary.

For most of the printed text on the brochure panels, I used Book Antigua or Arial Black fonts. Each time I mentioned *Hotels to Remember,* I used the Lucinda Calligraphy font for the title in keeping with the book cover font.

Using Microsoft Publisher to Create a Flyer

Often a one-page flyer printed back and front presents the best format for promoting a writer or artist. Carry it in a briefcase or portfolio, so that it may be placed flat on a table for use as a workshop or meeting handout.

To advertise some of my artwork, I created a one-page flyer using the Microsoft Publisher program. (See figures 3 and 4 at the end of this chapter.) One side featured two of my paintings taken from the My Images files. It also had a textbox on one side listing galleries where my work is shown and another textbox that featured biographical background. A sentence near the end stated I am available for commissioned artwork and for speaking engagements. Beneath that information my telephone number and e-mail address are listed.

The second side of the flyer featured "About the Author/Artist" biographical text plus a recent color photograph taken in one of my studio/galleries. Copies of two of my books were visible in the background.

Both this flyer and the three-panel brochure were printed in full color using a Hewlett-Packard DeskJet 5550. The 44-pound glossy Hewlett-Packard brochure and flyer paper works well.

It is not always necessary to use the more expensive glossy, or matte, brochure and flyer paper. For a display flyer that can also double as a poster for my novel, *Hearts Across Forever,* I used 90-pound index card stock. (See figure 5 at the end of this chapter.)

This very effective poster had a banner across the top with the book title, my name, the price, and the ISBN. It featured a photograph of two local tour guides at Rose Hall Great House in Jamaica where *Hearts Across Forever* was set.

A text box beneath the photograph gave a brief description of the story. A photograph of Rose Hall Great House was placed on the lower right side of the poster. A textbox in the middle noted the book was a 2002 PRISM Award finalist and that it won first place in another contest.

When placed in a heavy Plexiglas holder available at many computer supply stores, this poster proved ideal for book signings and other events. My holder also had a Plexiglas pocket perfect for displaying the three-panel brochures.

Creating a Media Kit

Whether you are an author or an artist, your goal must be to look professional in everything you do or say. That is especially important when you consider the appearance of your media kit.

Select a good quality laminated double-pocket folder to hold the items in your media kit. You will want to have some eye-catching business cards printed, or you can make them yourself using blank glossy photo business cards from Avery available at most office supply stores. Microsoft Publisher can help you create your own personalized full-color cards. The cards fit into slots on a pocket inside your folder.

Be sure to include copies of reviews for your books, especially ones from more prominent reviewers. My nonfiction book, *Hotels to Remember,* was reviewed by *Midwest Book Reviews, Southern Scribe, The Pen Woman, The Alumni Magazine for the College of William and Mary*, and a number of other publications. Remember to check Amazon for reviews you may want to include in your media kit.

A biographical sketch may also be included as well as photocopies of newspaper and magazine articles and photographs that feature you or your work. And you will need a dynamite press release about you and your work.

Creating an Impressive Press Release

Once again it is imperative that your press release looks professional. Check it carefully for spelling, grammatical, or content errors.

In the top left hand corner, type the words "FOR IMMEDIATE RELEASE." If you want it released on a specific date, type the release date. For example, "FOR RELEASE ON DECEMBER 25."

Beneath the FOR IMMEDIATE RELEASE, type the name of the contact person. That would be you or your publicist. A telephone number and an e-mail address should also be included.

Create a memorable title for your press release. You want to draw in the reader and spark the reader's imagination. The editor to whom you are sending this press release may substitute a new title or what you send may be the title used.

As you write your press release, remember the five "w's" of journalism: who, what, where, when, and why. At the end, type "30" or "The End." If you have more than one page, type "More" on the bottom of each page.

Remember, it is best to keep the press release to one page, if possible.

If you stir up enough interest or have an unusual topic, the book editor, reviewer, or reporter may want to interview you for a feature story.

If you have photos available, advise the editor that you can send photographs by e-mail or snail mail whichever is more convenient for the publication. Good photographs are always a plus.

A picture is worth a lot. And so is your creative imagination.

Design your brochures, flyers, business cards, media kits, press releases, and much more. Have fun. Make people aware of you and your products.

Side One, Brochure, *"Hotels to Remember"*

	Price on Request
HOTELS TO REMEMBER Autographed copy	
HEARTS ACROSS FOREVER Autographed copy	$8.95
6 SIGNED NOTECARDS from *HOTELS TO REMEMBER*	$15.00
Giclee Fine Art Prints from *HOTELS TO REMEMBER* Signed and numbered	$65.00
Please add $3.00 per book, card pack, or print shipping and handling.	$3.00

Check or money order to:

Mary Montague Sikes
P.O. Box 182
West Point, VA 23181

☆

Petersburg Regional Art Center
Petersburg, VA
Crossroads Art Center
Richmond, VA
Angel Hill Studio
West Point, VA 23181

Phone: 804-843-3284
Email: monti7clen@earthlink.net
www.alexnhudson.com

"The Jefferson Tower"
Giclee Fine Art Signed and Numbered Print
from *Hotels to Remember*
By Mary Montague Sikes

"a unique and breathtaking look at fabulous hotels around the world"
— Midwest Book Review

"entertaining to armchair travelers"
— 2003 VPW Communications Contest

"Each hotel exudes its own personality,"
Barbara Bell Matuszewski, The Pen Woman

"a beautiful table book featuring some of the grand hotels of the world."
— Southern Scribe

"Homestead," Hot Spring, VA
Giclee Fine Art Signed and Numbered Prints
"Williamsburg Inn," Williamsburg, VA

Side Two, Brochure, *"Hotels to Remember"*

MARY MONTAGUE SIKES

Exhibiting at:

Petersburg Regional Art Center,
Petersburg, VA
Art Works,
Richmond, VA
Angel Hill Studio
West Point, VA

Mary Montague Sikes is well known in Virginia and elsewhere as a painter, author, and journalist. She creates most of her art work in her studio in West Point, Virginia.

Sikes has a MFA degree in painting and printmaking from Virginia Commonwealth University. She studied sculpture under Carl Roseberg at the College of William and Mary.

A licensed teacher as well as an artist, Sikes offers painting workshops for children and adults. She is available for commissioned work and for speaking engagements.

For more information, she may be reached at
804-843-3284 or
monti7olen@earthlink.net

Visit Sikes' web site
http://www.alexishudson.com

Art Flyer, Side One

About Mary Montague Sikes

Mary Montague Sikes is a contemporary painter, journalist, freelance writer, art teacher, author of a published novel, *Hearts Across Forever*, and a coffee table book, *Hotels to Remember*. An award-winning photographer, her travel articles and photographs have appeared in magazines and newspapers across the country.

Her current works feature a series of abstract angel watercolors and a group of large fanciful tree acrylic paintings. Both her writing and artwork celebrate a positive outlook and a love of nature.

ART WORKS

Art Flyer, Side Two

HEARTS ACROSS FOREVER
By award-winning author
Mary Montague Sikes

$8.95

ISBN 1-892343-20-7

In Jamaica
Rose Hall tour guides are
thrilled to read
HEARTS ACROSS FOREVER,
award-winning novel,
by Mary Montague Sikes

2002
PRISM AWARD FINALIST
_First Place Winner
National Federation of Press
Women 2002 Communications
Contest_

_Long ago Rose Hall Great House
in Jamaica
was ruled by a wicked woman named
Annie Palmer.
Now Rose Hall Great House
is haunted by her ghost.
Read about her legend and how it affects
Catherine Calder, the heroine of_
HEARTS ACROSS FOREVER.

Poster for _"Hearts Across Forever"_

Original flyers and brochures are in color
for use at book signings and talks.

"'Tis a lesson you should heed,
Try, try again.
If at first you don't succeed,
Try, try again."

William E. Hickson, *Try and Try Again*

CHAPTER FIVE

Conducting Successful Book Signings

by Jean C. Keating

Book signings provide a unique opportunity for promoting your book. Signings bring the author together with your readers and with booksellers. The impact of these events far exceeds the amount of income derived from the sale of books during such signings.

What Book Signings Do for a Writer

- Create opportunities to meet readers and sell books
- Encourage booksellers to stock author's books

- Afford favorable location displays, if only short-term
- Provide publicity events for the book
- Provide opportunities to get to know store personnel

Book signings provide an opportunity for readers to acquire autographed copies of your book and to talk with you as an author. Each prospective buyer who comes to your table provides you as the author with opportunity to pitch your book. As you develop your skills in choosing the shortest and most appropriate description of your book to interest the individual involved, you are also honing your skills at describing your book to radio show announcers and other booksellers. You're learning and growing as you work.

Signings provide you with a lot of quality time in a bookstore in which to get to know store personnel and their routines, to talk with them about subjects pertaining to book sales and fluctuating market demands. These contacts provide the opportunity to improve future business relationships with the particular store as well as other stores, and are a fine opportunity to ask questions that will help you develop your marketing skills, such as: How have sales of your type of book been in the past year? How have sales been in the past month? What seems to attract their readers to books of your type?

While successful sales are a primary objective of book signings, other benefits are equally important. Any appearance or signing provides an opportunity for publicity, even if it is just a line in an events calendar in the newspaper. If you find a way to make the news of a book signing key to something else going on in the community or town, there is more of an opportunity to attract a bigger story and publicity for your book.

Depending on other activities within a store during the time of the signing or a reading, an author gains a choice display space for a time, be it only a few hours before and during the book signing. Consider the money expended by major publishing houses to obtain highly visible floor spots for their displays of new books by top name authors! An author favored with a book signing has "center stage" for a brief time in that store for the price of the arrangements and the time devoted to the signing. Make the most of it.

Moreover, stores that are allowed to do their own buying will always keep a few of your books for their shelves after your signings. Many readers return after book signings and decide they want to buy the book they've seen at the signing, or decide they want additional copies for gifts after reading the first one.

Authors' Events

Book signings draw larger crowds when they are combined with readings (most effective with poetry and fiction), or with workshops and seminars (effective with non-fiction books). Events, which include readings or workshops along with signing books, usually draw bigger crowds and attract even more attention to your book, but require more effort at publicity and promotion. [See Chapter 4.]

Getting Publisher Scheduled Book Signings

When publishers organize book tours for their authors, these events can cost $1,000 or more per day, since the publisher pays transportation and lodging for the author if you're one of the special classes mentioned earlier (you remember: a former president or first lady). A first-time or trying-to-be-famous author can often get a publisher to arrange author appearances and signings by providing a line-of-intended travel on a vacation trip or some other plans for travel. The publisher won't pay anything for transportation or lodging, but they will arrange a series of appearances at booksellers along the way.

You can further promote your book by contacting other booksellers along your route of travel and arranging additional signings at these alternate booksellers yourself.

Scheduling Book Events for Yourself

- Start with your local stores.
- Analyze what types of books they carry.
- Contact them by phone.
- Make certain they have sufficient books for the sale and for a satisfactory looking display.
- Discuss publicity plans with the store.

- Plan for a prop.
- Arrange for an icebreaker.
- Provide bookmarks.

If your publisher won't arrange publicity events for you or if you are your own publisher, you should begin your work with local booksellers. These are the most convenient and the least expensive to work with since they require no lodging or travel expenses while you develop your skills at doing it yourself. Moreover, these are the stores most likely to be interested in you because of your local presence, which translates into friends and family who will support your store appearance.

First, determine the types of booksellers in your community and the books they carry. You won't get far calling a store about a signing of a new romance if they carry only children's books or they only carry out-of-print and reduced priced books. If there is more than one bookseller in your area for your type of book, scan your local paper for announcements of book events and make your first call to the one that seems to offer the most promotion and announcements.

Contact the store by phone. Say that you are a local author and would like to speak to whoever deals with local authors. Be ready to tell the store contact the essential facts about your book: a brief description, the audience it should attract, the price and general description (paperback, hardback, pictures if any) in about 50 short, strong, and well-prepared words. Follow up any arrangements with a letter restating everything.

Don't forget about places other than bookstores in planning these signings. Read carefully the chapter on niche marketing, and include places of interest in your particular book in your list of locations to call about signings.

My books are related to dogs: a mystery, a collection of short stories, and a memoir of life over two decades and six generations of dogs in which the voice of the author alternates with whimsical letters written by the dogs. I look for places that sell *new* books on fiction, mystery, dogs, humor, and life stories to name a few. In addition to bookstores in my hometown, my books are available in an upscale pet store, which sells doggie and people clothing, doggie biscuits, pet games, and such. My books are also in the local Barnes and Noble store with about 100,000 other books. Do you even need to guess in which place my books get the more favorable exposure or sell more often?

Make certain the bookseller obtains enough books for the appearance to provide a pleasing display. Usually 20 books are sufficient for the table display; other things to attract potential readers also should be on the table.

Discuss publicity plans with the store manager. Usually each store has a routine of inserting a few lines in the community calendar of the event. A more effective plan for publicity is to get the store to agree to do its own publicity for the event. You should also prepare and send to newspapers an announcement from you or your publisher that will give a broader description of the planned appearance.

Along with your letter confirming arrangements, you should provide a written bio as well as a brief (250 -300 words) description of your book. If possible, at least three weeks ahead of your appearance provide the store with 100 copies of a flyer containing at least a graphic of the book cover, your bio, and the brief description of your book. Ask to have the flyer placed around the store, or inserted in outgoing packages during the weeks before your appearance.

Now think in terms of how to utilize your brief time in the limelight. Your book will be out in a highly visible location in the store for a short period, not sitting on a shelf with the spine out along with hundreds or thousands of other books. Think how to attract potential buyers to your book. Plan carefully what you use for the display board and any other prop that will draw potential buyers to that display table and to your book. At the very least, have a 14" by 20" poster of your book cover. Have it made so that a small poster of the event time and date can be attached and replaced for future events. One friend uses a stuffed dog that is 28 inches high beside a large poster of her book cover to promote her book about her pet malamute's battle with cancer. The eye-catching display draws people of all ages to her table and books.

The day of the signing, arrange to have some sort of an icebreaker on the table. A small dish of wrapped candies invites people to come up and take one. I use, when I can, one of my tiny, live dogs because I write dog-related mysteries, short stories, and novels. My current signing partner is a five-pound papillon named Puff. He has numerous personas, and varies them according to local events and conditions. At mystery conventions, he goes as Sherlock Bones. For Christmas readings, he appears with me as Little Santa Paws. When we attended a book signing in connection with the Blackbeard festival, he dressed in black silk and magenta satin as Blackears the Pirate. Whatever your niche, you want something to attract people to your table, and give you the opportunity to engage them in conversation.

Lastly, always have something for them to take away even if they don't buy your book right then. Bookmarks are inexpensive to produce in black and white on colored paper. Put a graphic of the book cover and print information on the bookmark showing title, author, price, a brief description of your book and where it is available. Consider having enough bookmarks made to leave in the store. Work with the store. Ask them first if free bookmarks are acceptable. Sometimes stores sell bookmarks and don't want your free ones to conflict with their sales. Usually, a store welcomes the freebies. If free bookmarks are acceptable, ask the store personnel to put one in each bag of book purchases from their store. It's a very effective way of promoting your book to people who are regular purchasers of books.

A Word of Caution

Start tomorrow. And don't be discouraged if your first signing doesn't bring the hordes of buyers that some marketing books promise. Actually, bookstores are very happy if a signing without a reading sells ten books. That is just the beginning of the game of promoting your book to the reading public. At the first signing of my first book, I sold 71 copies. All my friends and fellow writers turned out *en masse* to make it a big success. I was a bit embarrassed that so few people other than friends bought my books, but I was invited back enthusiastically for a second signing by the storeowner. My second signing brought only 17 sales, and I was crushed. When the manager asked me back for a third time, I stammered an apology about the lack of sales and admitted I thought he was just being polite in asking me back for a third time. He quickly set me straight. He said he was never nice—with a little grin that said otherwise—and quoted several other book events with far better known authors where the sales totaled only four books. The one thing he impressed upon me was that author's events sell books, if not the ones to be autographed, other books in the store; if not at the time of the signings, when customers return at a later time.

So you have nothing to lose but time. Get on that phone and schedule a signing or a reading.

Here's Puff as the Virginia Cavalier at my book signing table.

CHAPTER SIX

Getting the Word Out About Your Book

by Jean C. Keating

There are many ways to spread the word that your book is published and available for sale. Two ways that many writers think of first are advertisements in magazines and newspapers and arrangements with companies that specialize in providing publicity support. While this may work for companies with big bucks to spend who are unwilling to devote in-house staff to do publicity, it has not been the way to go for me as a writer and small publisher. I have had much better results from less expensive, more tightly structured ways of publicizing my books. Consider the eight that are discussed below.

- A website, which discusses my books and allows interested parties to review, contact me for information and comments, and buy my books.
- A signature line to all my Internet mail that directs people to my website and briefly showcases prestigious awards my books achieve.
- Entries in relevant writing contests for the books.
- Press releases of general interest to the reading public that are about my dogs or some funny event that just happens to mention my books or book signings.
- Donations of books as raffle prizes to help organizations whose memberships are consistent with my topic.
- Combining book signings with events to support my favorite charities and donating part of the sales to that charity.
- Providing free gifts to people who stop by my book signing table or attend lectures and presentations.
- Making and wearing T-shirts displaying the cover of my book on the front.

Publicity and Marketing Firms

Many publicity and marketing firms are very expensive, offering packages that start around $3500-$5000 and go up from there. The companies indicate they will promote your work to the book clubs, gain you reviews in Publisher's Weekly and all the big reviewer

names. It sounds like just what you need.
Right?
Wrong!
These companies want the money up
front. They talk in generalities. They offer no
guarantee. They sidestep providing deadlines for
their efforts.

What these companies offer, stripped of
the flowery language, is to send your book along
with an announcement, which you will have to
write and rewrite for them until it is finally
correct, to these book clubs, reviewers and such.
Being gullible, I fell for it: ONCE! I did insist on
having a list of the addresses to which the
notices, announcements, letters, and books were
sent. When nothing happened, the publicity
company wanted more money for following up
on the original submissions. So I sent the follow-
ups with my return address on them. More than
37% were faulty addresses, which were returned
as undeliverable.

A larger problem arose. Many of the
addresses to which the publicity firm sent free
books not only never provided reviews, but
raised my suspicions that they asked for free
books for the sole purpose of getting them to sell
on amazon.com and on e-Bay. Why am I
paranoid? Well, I was a 'rocket scientist' in my
first career, so when I put two and two together
and get four I call it like I see it. Before I ever
released books, there were fourteen copies for
sale at cut prices on amazon.com. The only
release of books other than to my storage facility
at that time had been to a publicity/marketing
firm in New York City. The only source of the

books other than those sitting in my warehouse, were the ones shipped originally to the publicity firm. So when fourteen turned up on amazon.com at cut rate prices, the only source of the books was through the publicity firm to addresses that were supposed to provide reviews! Not exactly what I'd assumed I was paying for.

The only review attained by the high priced publicity firm was with Midwest Book Review. I had attained a review with that delightful group [who are wonderful about supporting independent publishers] for my two previous books by contacting them myself.

Paid Advertisements

In most magazines and newspapers, advertisements not only cost a lot of money but are like commercials on television. Unless you're determined to sit through commercials in the hopes of viewing another "wardrobe malfunction"—which isn't too likely given the stiff fines now being proposed by the FCC—you ignore the commercials and wait for the return of your program. In much the same way, paid advertisements not only cost a lot of money but also are never as effective as a good article in the same magazine or newspaper about your book, about yourself, which just happens to mention your book, or about a niche-related topic, which just happens to mention your book.

Advertisements in publications can and do work, but it takes experimenting with ad layouts, working to understand the audience, and paying constant attention to trends within the advertising venture. Start small and learn what works before you gamble on expensive ads. Review returns and be brutal about the bottom line, returns from identifiable sales relating to the advertising compared to costs.

A good news story is worth any twenty paid ads in my experience. One very effective way of getting the word out about your book is to develop a press release that provides something newsworthy that you can send to local papers in connection with your signing. A sound understanding of the information needed in a news item coupled with careful consideration of information of interest to the readers can lead to wonderful coverage by local newspapers. It will increase the attendance at your book signings, improve sales before and after at the bookstore, boost sales on amazon.com. and lead to invitations for future signings and appearances.

Your Website

This is the twenty-first century and you can't expect to function in it without a website to present yourself and your books to the world. Carl and Jenny Loveland have provided an extensive discussion in Chapter 13 about designing and developing your website. My comments in this chapter will focus on my experiences with ways to direct traffic to your website.

One important thing to remember in directing traffic to your website is the short shelf-life of any technique. As an example, let me share my experiences with pop-up banners as a means of promoting your book. When I published my first book in 1998, a friend who maintained the lottery information website for California, New York, Texas and Virginia gave me free pop-up ads as a present on my new career. I got over 200 orders for my book before it was ever published. So when I published my second book in 2001, I tried pop-up banners again. I got no sales or hits on my website from those banners. In three short years, pop-up banners had ceased to be novel and attention getting and had become annoying instead. So be alert for changes and change with the times in keeping abreast of the latest means of utilizing the computer to promote your books.

Signature Line on E-mails

In this day and age, most of us belong to numerous list-serves, lists of like-minded individuals who correspond frequently about subjects of joint interest to subscribers. Moreover, such lists are developing and expanding every day. To use this form of publicizing your book requires no money. You need only consider who are likely to be your most interested group of readers. If you're writing about what you know, chances are you're already a member of lists that are the primary interest group for your book.

I write fiction that features a little breed of dog called a papillon. When I joined a list-serve of papillon fanciers in 1993, there were only 70 odd members on the list because this small dog was not generally known by the public. List members then and now correspond daily and sometimes several times a day about food, medication, behavior problems, travel difficulties, training issues, you name it. In 1999, a black-and-white beauty named CH Loteki's Supernatural Being [called Kirby] won the triple crown of dog shows: Best in Show at the World show, the Canadian Invitational and the Westminster Kennel Club. Interest in the breed skyrocketed. The original papillon list spawned four additional Internet lists. Membership on the original expanded to four figures and the four new lists were equally popular. Like most Internet list-serves, advertising is prohibited on the list. However, no restrictions apply to a signature line or lines. And every e-mail that I send or answer, including e-mail to these special interest groups, carries the signature line below, updated and augmented with the newest attainments by my books.

Jean

Jean C. Keating
author of Amorous Accident [a dog mystery featuring a
Papillon named Sky],
Pawprints On My Heart, finalist for national DWAA award as
best dog fiction of 2001
and Paw Prints Through The Years, finalist for national
DWAA and Merial Award as best work describing the human-
animal bond for 2004
Williamsburg, VA
www.Astrapublishers.com

Book Contests

Utilize Internet browsers to find book competitions that fit your type and subject of book. Then enter as many as you can that fit your topic and niche. The cost of such endeavors is minimal: your time and effort in entering the book, one or several copies of your book (which gets copies into the hands of people who have similar interests), the entrance fee (which may range from $10 to $50), and the postage. In return, your book may win or become one of two or three finalists for a national award, which isn't bad publicity. You can brag about that in your future publicity flyers, press releases, and in your signature line as I've shown above. Moreover, your book is seen by individuals who may be editors or publishers in your field.

When my second book competed for the national award by Dog Writers' Association of America (DWAA) for best dog fiction in 2001, it was one of four national finalists. It didn't win. The Maxwell medallion went to a Canadian author, Gail MacMillan, for her mystery, *Biography of A Beagle*. But as a results of that competition, I got an offer from the publishers of *Romantic Times BOOKclub Magazine* to do a feature story on DWAA winners. I could not have afforded a paid ad in this four-color photo quality paper magazine. The resulting half-page spread shown below appeared in the September 2003 issue of the magazine. It featured my byline as well as a review of my mystery,

Amorous Accident. All this resulted from my decision to enter my second book in best dog fiction competition. Needless to say, this article brought a big boost in sales of my book on Amazon and on my website, since this is a top national magazine for promoting romance and mystery books.

The Dog Writers of America's Canine Cannon

READERS OF THE CANINE CANNON know Susan Conant, Laurien Berensen, Carole Lea Benjamin—all credited with popularizing dogs as major characters in fiction. But these authors have a growing number of colleagues in the Dog Writers Association of America (**www.dwaa.org**). Started in 1935 with a handful of people drawn together by a common interest in dogs and writing, the association today has an annual writing competition that attracts international interest and features a best dog fiction category. Here's a look at past finalists and winners sent in by DWAA member, Jean C. Keating.

AMOROUS ACCIDENT: A DOG'S EYE VIEW OF MURDER JEAN C. KEATING
This first mystery by NASA engineer and Papillon breeder turned writer features amateur sleuth/engineer Genna Kingsley and her Papillon, Sky. Genna and Sky are called to assist with the murder investigation of a prominent research doctor. Her husband's godfather, a homicide lieutenant, discovers two canine eyewitnesses, and he wants Genna to use the dogs' responses to find the killer. Available from Astra Publishers, **www.astrapublishers.com**.

BIOGRAPHY OF A BEAGLE GAIL MACMILLAN
With seven published romance novels to her credit, Gail MacMillan proves equally talented in recounting her love affair with a swashbuckling little canine rake named Brandy. Brandy races from one grand adventure to the next, happily letting Gail explain, cajole and sometimes fib him out of his next predicament. Winner of the DWAA Maxwell Award for Best Dog Fiction of 2001. Available from Borealis Press, **www.borealispress.com**.

BUDDY & THE JACK W. BRYAN SMITH
Smith's first novel is about Buddy, a mongrel blinded through abuse and left homeless, scared and alone. Trapped in a dark world and terrorized by feral cats, Buddy is saved by Jack, a homeless but fearless Jack Russell terrier who leads him on a search for a loving home. The support and love shared by the two unfortunate dogs is echoed by a romantic subplot involving humans. Available from America House Book Publishers, **www.publisheramerica.com**.

HOWLING BLOODY MURDER SUE OWENS WRIGHT
Wright's delightful first novel introduces fortysomething half-Washoe Indian "Beanie" MacBean and her basset hound, Cruiser. When a bitter dispute between land developers and the Washoe turns to murder, Beanie and Cruiser try to sniff out the killer. Available from Deadly Alibi Press, **www.deadlyalibipress.com**.

MINGA, A LOVE STORY ARLIE ALFORD TOYE
More than a century ago, deep in the English Midlands, four miniature bulldog puppies—Minga, Tig, Farley and Daffodil—are sold to different owners and embark on new lives filled with unknown dangers and human agendas. With spirit and tenacity, they face astonishing odds, attempting the most incredible of feats. In doing so, they touch the hearts of those they meet along the way. Brimming with suspense, adventure and humor, this is also a love story that will touch your heart. Available from ARDesigns, Inc., **www.ardesigninc.com**.

VOICES OF THE DOGS AT THE WESTMINSTER DR. LOUIS VINE
After receiving a sharp crack on the head, the Westminster veterinarian can suddenly converse with the dogs at the show. The compassionate and intriguing dialogue sparked by this premise allows for a delightful mix of humor and entertainment, combined with information about the activities at this world-famous show. This delightful page-turner was a finalist for best dog fiction in 2002. Available from 1st Books Library, **www.1stbooks.com**.

The graphic shown above is used with the kind permission of Ms. Carol Stacy, Publisher & Internet Director for *Romantic Times BOOKclub Magazine*. It appeared as the bottom half of page 17 in the September 2003 issue

Press Releases

In the preceding chapter, I talked briefly about developing press releases to augment your book signings. You're a wordsmith, so first concentrate on what makes a newspaper want to print a story, and then carefully observe the basics of a good newspaper article: who, when, where, why, and what.

A book signing is worthy of a news story if you're a former president, a big name celebrity, or a big-time crook. If you're a struggling to-be-discovered, beginning or mid-line writer, you've got to provide something of more interest to a newspaper's readership to get a story, something that grabs the attention of the paper's reading public.

Think about the niche into which your book fits. What would appeal to the newspaper's readers that might like your book? Now find something that you can link to your signing that will be appealing to those readers and write it up in a way that will impress a newspaper editor.

Ask your local coordinator – the bookstore owner, the program chairman for your appearance—for the names of three of four newspapers that serve the area. Prepare press releases for these three or four papers about something related to but not restricted to your signing or appearance. If at all possible have some attention-getting photograph that you can include. Call each paper and tell them you have a special interest article you'd like to submit and get the name of the person to whom it should be addressed. Ask for their publication schedule, and their deadline for receiving such an article. Some of the best coverage you will get with such efforts will come from small presses who publish twice weekly or weekly.

Let me share with you some examples of how this has worked for me with my dog books.

My appeal is first and foremost to dog lovers, secondly to people who love a good mystery. I first trained one of my dogs to pose in costumes and developed several personas for him: Sherlock Bones, the Virginia Cavalier (you saw this picture in the previous chapter), Blackeared the Pirate, and Little Santa Paws. I had the costumes custom made for him so each would be a special story in and of itself. Then I had suitably staged professional photographs made of him in his four personae, making certain that I had copyright releases enabling me to utilize these photos in my publicity efforts.

Next, I developed a special interest story about the dog and his special persona and costume coming to visit. I included amusing information about his costume and some of the problems with developing it. I also included a lengthy bio of myself and of Puff. I sent this extensive press release along with an 8 x 10-color photograph of Puff (he's much better looking than I) to each of my selected newspaper contacts. Out of every four papers, one published the photo and compete press release, two published the picture and an abbreviated news story, and only one published an abbreviated story without the photo.

Donate to Raffles

There are many opportunities to publicize your book by donating a copy for raffles or door prizes at functions where the attendees are likely to be interested in your genre. I get numerous requests from humane societies, dog clubs, and animal welfare groups for free copies of my books. I am happy to contribute. It means my book or books are displayed for people attending to view, bid on, and talk about.

Combine book signings with events to support your favorite charity

This is a great way to promote your book and help groups you want to support at the same time. By giving the group part of the proceeds, you can help yourself and the charity.

Given my chosen area of writing, you can guess that I'm passionate about support to animals. So when I was asked to help an SPCA's effort with their fund to build a shelter, you can bet I jumped at the chance. I arranged to come and do a reading and a signing, bringing my little sidekick Puff in his persona as Little Santa Paws since the event was scheduled for mid-November. Half the sales price of each book sold went to the SPCA's building fund.

When you combine donations to local charities with the special efforts in creating a newsworthy story, you get wonderful help from local papers. One such press release, from the *Mecklenburg Sun,* in Clarksville, Virginia is shown on the next page. Not only did the *Mecklenburg Sun* publish my entire press release with the picture I provided to them, but they sent a photographer to the event, took several pictures of their own, and published their pictures with a brief credit on their editorial page in the next issue of their paper.

Getting the Word Out About Your Book

Wednesday, November 17, 2004   The Mecklenburg Sun

Santa Paws Is Coming To Town

Santa Paws

The R.T. Arnold Library will host a special visitor on Friday, Nov. 19. Santa Paws will be appearing from 10 a.m.-2 p.m. at the library at 111 East Danville in South Hill. A little five-pound Papillon named Puff (Astra's Coffee'NCream) will accompany his author/owner for a book signing and pawgraphing session at that time.

A preview of Santa Paws' gift-loaded sleigh was captured by Denise Hilton in his red velvet and whit fur costume — a dog-size version of Santa's with red coat and pants, green waistcoat, and tall hat with bell. His costumer chuckled at the challenge of creating a hat that would be visible when set between the huge butterfly ears of the tiny dog and not be too have for a head described as "two fleas wide and a half-a-grasshopper long."

Santa Paws' owner, Jean C. Keating, has been writing novels starring companion animals for five years. At the request of South Hill resident, Mrs. William Ladd, Keating and Santa Paws are coming to South Hill for a book signing and sale to benefit the library. Residents can avail themselves of holiday presents suitable for ages ten to ninety-nine with half the purchase going to benefit the library.

Twice during the period, Santa Paws will assist his owner in a presentation of their two meetings with a real life Santa. Readings of a story entitled "I Believe" will take place from 11 to 11:30 and from 1:00 to 1:30 p.m. in the library meeting room. The humorous tale honors a Williamsburg native who gave much of his time to support the Heritage Humane Society with appearances as Santa Claus and

ended up saving Santa Paws' ancestor when she was lost in a snow storm.

On Friday evening, Nov. 19, Santa Paws and his owner will be the guests at an invitation-only wine and cheese and meet-the-author gathering in Clarksville at The Mariposa Cafe, where the book signing and reservation fees will benefit the Clarksville SPCA. This event is being sponsored by The Mariposa Cafe, Century 21 on the Lake, Simmons & Assoc. Realty, Inc.

In 2004 Keating was nominated for a Pulitzer Prize for "Paw Prints Through The Years." This third and latest book by Keating has also been nominated for numerous other national and state awards including the Library of Virginia Literary Award, a National Book Award and Dog Writers' Association of America's Maxwell Award for Best Dog Fiction.

Keating's second book, "Pawprints On My Heart," was one of three finalists for Best Dog Fiction of 2001.

Puff, in his persona of Sherlock Bones, started helping out with book signing appearances with Keating's first book, a mystery featuring a Papillon named Sky. The canine ham continued his efforts with an appearance on a national panel with his owner to talk about the roles of animals in mysteries.

Keating holds degrees in Mathematics, Physics and Information Systems. Named Virginia's Outstanding Young Woman of the Year in 1970 for her civic as well as professional efforts as an aerospace engineer with NASA, she authored more than 50 scientific and educational administrative reports during her years with NASA and subse-

quent service as head of Research for Virginia's Higher Education Council.

Keating retired from government service in 1998 and began writing fiction. Her first two published books include the mystery set in Williamsburg and Richmond and a collection of short stories about animal companions. Her latest novel chronicles the loves and laughs of living with six generations of her dogs. The voice of the author alternates with whimsical holiday letters from the dogs in which they present their own versions of the human-animal bond. Keating's short stories have been published in "Pap Pourri,"

"The Write Dog," "RT Booknotes" and four editions of "Critique's Choice." She is a regular contributor to "Animal Antics" for Chesapeake Style Magazine.

Santa Paws' handsome picture has appeared on the covers of several magazines including "The Write Dog," the national magazine for Dog Writers' Association of America and "Chesapeake Style Magazine."

You can meet them both at the R.T. Arnold Library on Nov. 19 from 10 a.m.-2 p.m. and in Clarksville from 5-7 p.m. at The Mariposa Cafe, pick up some Christmas presents and benefit some worthy causes at the same time.

News article published by the Mecklenburg Sun, November 17, 2004

Coverage such as this article is invaluable in your press kits, to your future sales, and to your ego. And best of all, I got a lovely thank you from the group telling me all the animals that this fundraiser help to save. A win-win situation all around!

Paw Prints

Astra's Coffee and Cream, aka "Puff" signs his owner's book at a Lake Country SPCA fundraiser held at the Mariposa Café in Clarksville Friday. Author Jean Keating was the guest at "Pawprints Through the Years" book signing and sale. Some of the proceeds from the sale of the book went to the SPCA. (Valerie Garrison photo)

The Mecklenburg Sun

Editorial

Wednesday, November 24, 2004

Photos and text used with permission of Tom McLaughlin, Editor, *Meckhlenburg Sun,* Clarksville, Virginia from editorial page of paper dated November 24, 2004.

Free Gifts

Never miss an opportunity to leave a free gift with people who attend your signings or lectures. Hold some little contest and give away one of your books. Or have bookmarks showing your book or books covers, your website and acquisition information (as mentioned in the previous chapter). Or simply print a brief excerpt or poem from your book, if copyright rules allow it, and give to attendees.

I found that the brief introduction to one of my books was something that attendees at my signings and readings appreciated, so I started making black-and-white copies and giving them away. These freebies were well-received and everyone had something to take home to remind them of my books and me—with a suitable notation of my website on the gift of course.

They give so much, and ask so little, these companions in fur.
They offer uncompromising love, the warmth of total acceptance.
They live in the moment, expressing their joy at our company
    with unabashed devotion.
They teach us when we let them, to enjoy the here and now.
They comfort when we are distressed and are joyful at our
happiness.
They need us, give us focus; give us a reason to go on.
During their all too brief passage through our lives,
    they leave paw prints on clothes and carpets, on hearth and
    home.
Even when their earthly journey is over, the memories of their
pranks, companionship, and love enrich our lives as long
    as we live.
May there always be Pawprints On My Heart.

— by Jean C. Keating
    from the book: Pawprints On My Heart
    Astra Publishers: ISBN 0-9674016-1-5
    www.Astrapublishers.com

T-Shirts

Last, but certainly not least, consider being your own walking billboard. Have several t-shirts made featuring the cover of your book. Wear them to all events where casual wear is appropriate. You'll get lots of questions and friendly inquiries. And it won't cost you a penny of your marketing budget; it is all chargeable to your wardrobe budget isn't it?

So start carefully defining your niche, the groups to which your work is most likely to appeal, and try some of these ways to get the word out about your book.

CHAPTER SEVEN

Selling Your Books by Speaking in Public

by E.R. Kallus and Mildred H. B. Roberson

It's hard to conceive a more potent marketing package than an author selling a book, the artistic product of his imagination and skill. What better way to create excitement in your book than to tell readers about it? Buzzing, hyping, marketing, or just plain selling. No matter what it may be called, this is still about you, your book, and your skill with words. It can be as simple and easy as describing your book to an acquaintance, or as complex as spending thousands of dollars on a big-time publicist.

When you can answer the question, "What have you been doing with yourself?" by saying, "I've written a book," you can be assured of an immediate audience. There's something irresistible in learning about a person who has written a book and the very personal process of writing it. That's the plain and simple reason why speaking in public is an author's most potent tool for selling a book.

Me, A Public Speaker?

In Chapter Two, we acknowledged that many first time authors have become accustomed to thinking of themselves as shy and retiring. That's probably because the solitary nature of forging their thoughts into sentences and paragraphs in a quiet, uninterrupted atmosphere. The mere thought of emerging from the quiet and warmth of their writing places to speak in public makes them fearful.

If you're one of those, try looking at yourself as your neighbor might. To anyone who isn't a writer, you're an extrovert, someone whose thoughts are so urgent that you've set them down on paper. And far more than that, your words are printed, in a bright, shiny cover and available for sale.

Now, to most people, that's an unmistakable act of confidence. So you've actually taken the first step in publicizing your work. Build on that. All you have to do is tell that neighbor about your book in such a way that she'll want to buy it. From that point, it's only a small step to sharing your story with groups of people who are interested in the same things that motivated you to write your book. The thing to remember about public speaking is that the most difficult obstacle to clear is convincing yourself to share your work. Once you've done that, it's easy.

Where Do I Begin?

The answer to that questions is, begin by working from your strength. Talk to groups of people who are likely to be interested in hearing about what you know best: yourself, your book and your motivation for writing it.

Let's use Mildred H. B. Roberson's book, *My Bag Was Always Packed* as an example. She's a retired professor of nursing who's written a biography, the story told by Claudine Curry Smith an African-American lay midwife who practiced her critical art in a remote, rural area located on a peninsula thrusting into the Chesapeake on the western shore of Virginia. It's a powerful human-interest story of intense motivation and perseverance, bringing children safety into the world under extremely trying conditions where, if it had not been for Mrs. Smith, the mothers might have gotten no official help at all.

Who wouldn't want to hear Mildred talk about the book and how she wrote it with the amazing midwife herself? But the better question is, "Who would?" Getting the word out originates with finding a receptive audience. If you're familiar with internet searches, think how you structure your queries and work backwards. Begin by making a list of keywords that would bring you to the subject that Mildred and Mrs. Smith wrote about, and you have a good starting point for finding affinity groups interested in the book and how it was written. You'd find nurses and other groups of medical professionals, historians (medical, Virginia, local, and African-American), sociologists, and people who want a good story about coping with life in rural America.

Just take a quick look at the Internet for professional affinity groups. If your book is based on your career experiences, you can probably find dozens of organizations and associations, local and national. They're all seeking speakers. The same principle applies if your books are about pets. Crime solver books would appeal to law enforcement organizations, and books on hotels to travel agents, but you get the idea.

Let's say that you're a member of a professional organization whose interests are linked with the subject of your book like Mildred's is. Start with them. If not, try some of the local civic clubs like the Chamber of Commerce or the Lions Clubs as a start. They're eager, energetic, and they'll be receptive to what you say. Another positive aspect of going to them is that they always need speakers, and you, by choosing well, might be opening your public speaking sales campaign before an audience of people you know.

Start small, be persistent but aggressive and, as you improve your presentation, you'll be able to speak to larger and larger events and sell your books faster. Put the daunting prospect of speaking on the radio off until you feel comfortable with speaking and with your message.

As you continue to speak, you'll want to increase the scope of your audiences. The obvious progression, of course, is to arrange your speaking engagements at larger and larger events. Don't be surprised that as you become better and better at your presentation, word of mouth publicity will result in more opportunities to speak.

One point to consider in your planning: Many of the local organizations like civic and church organizations meet in a setting that involves a breakfast before going to work or to church. Consider that no matter how interesting your presentation might be, at some point your listeners' attention may shift to their next appointment. One by one, they'll find themselves sustained by their breakfast, entertained by your remarks and focused upon getting to work or cleaning up the hall to get into the church on time. They might think that to slow down to buy your book takes time they already have allocated.

Unless you keep your audience interested and your eye on the clock, the last words you may hear are, "Sure enjoyed your talk. Need any help carrying those books out to the car?" Make arrangements beforehand to be certain you have an opportunity to sell your books.

Am I Ready To Speak In Public?

Let's pause right here to take stock. Nothing we're writing about public speaking should be taken to mean that you shouldn't immediately go straight to radio or television to sell your books. In fact, we strongly urge you to step up the aggressiveness of your marketing program whenever you feel comfortable in doing so. We do suggest that, in beginning, it might be a good idea to start close to home, particularly if you truly are one of those to whom speaking in public doesn't come easily. But we think that, with either route you choose in taking your first steps, the principles of preparation are identical.

If your presentation is polished and doesn't need any practice before a neighborly audience, it might be worth the effort to set your sights high at the beginning, so that you appear as the featured speaker with a stage and a lectern and an audience primed to hear about your book—and to buy copies of it.

What Will I Say?

When you stand before the audience you arranged to address, your purpose will be to sell your book, but a good way to begin is by selling yourself. An author we know is an example. She tells her audience about her early days in the Coast Guard when she commanded a small cutter patrolling the Pacific waters near Catalina. She and her crew were notified to look for a certain suspicious yacht, thought to be a drug runner and told to stop it if they could and take over with an armed boarding party. Her audiences wait on the edges of their chairs to hear about what they're sure to come.

"We saw the yacht," she says, "and called for them to stop, but they didn't." She tells of preparing the cutter's machine gun to fire a single shot across the bow of the yacht and anticipation rises, and finally of ordering her gunner to fire that single shot. She has their undivided attention. "In his excitement, he fired automatic burst that nearly sawed the bow off that yacht," she says with an impish grin. That's when she transitions gracefully with the information that her real purpose in speaking is to tell them about her book. It's a cookbook, of all things, and it features the recipes of superbly trained cooks aboard Coast Guard vessels.

Not every author has a story like that to tell, but something from your experiences could be just as powerful in beginning your presentation. Here are some additional thoughts for those whose experiences are not so uniquely connected to their books.

Why not tell your listeners what impelled you to write the book in the first place? You'll find that readers are fascinated by the reasons authors give for starting a book. One of our collaborators has written a book based on stories told to him by an old friend. He overheard the older man telling the story of the colonel of a cavalry regiment presiding over a festive dinner in a large hall. In a planned show of élan, the colonel had a horse brought to the hall—a horse shod with rubber horseshoes. To the thunderous applause of almost everyone in the hall, the colonel proceeded to jump the horse over the heads of seated diners, table after table. Only the regimental physician took offense at having a horse's hooves fly close overhead. Stories like this are very powerful in answering the question, "What inspired me to write this story?"

Another way to begin, if you don't have stories like these, is to step right up and talk about your book itself. Maybe you think of your book as a much more thoughtful literary work than books about midwives, horse cavalry, and cooking aboard ships smashing their way through the Arctic sea lanes. Just remember that a writer's job is to capture humanity, and you've just published your written thoughts. We remind you that what you've accomplished is extraordinary in itself, and you need only to prepare yourself well and then tell your story.

It can be a good idea to select a single chapter of your book, especially if it introduces a particularly interesting character. If it's in a work of non-fiction, say a travel book, you may want to concentrate on a single historic site like the majestic roman bridge across the Tagus River in Spain's Extremadura Province.

Joe Guion, another of the contributors to this book, has written a book of poems. No other genre evokes more introspection and emotion in its readers than poetry does. Most of us will agree that though most conversations between an author and an acquaintance will touch quickly on "What's it about?" it's a little different with a poet. With these special writers, listeners' curiosities veer in another direction. It's a little more specific. "Why do you write poetry?"

Think about referring to how you go about crafting the opening words of your book. What was so interesting to you that the story just crackled off your fingertips and onto the keys of your word processor?

Many will want to know how you write. If you don't mention it in your presentations, expect questions about how you organize your day or how you maintain your focus. Frequently, people will want to know how much you're capable of writing in a day. Don't simply tell them that the key to prolific writing is to keep your tail in the seat and don't get up until you're done. Here again is a place you can make points on a question that is almost sure to arise. Be ready to tell them how you write, but don't grope for words while you do it. Do you wear a baseball cap or a favorite sweater to tell yourself that serious writing is to be done? Maybe you begin with a writing drill such as composing a paragraph of the best dialogue you can devise.

One more thing must not be ignored any further. What if you honed your presentation to perfection and impressed your audience, but you forgot to ask them to buy your book? This is truly critical. *Never* forget that your primary reason for speaking in public is to interest readers in your book and not necessarily to sell it on the spot. You should not lose an opportunity to convert the audience into buyers. Let's put that another way. Don't forget that you came to sell your books.

Preparation

Earlier, we suggested that organizations are quite open to a variety of speakers, but that's not to say that they will embrace an unprepared speaker. You won't know you haven't met their expectations until afterward.

So how does an author become a speaker? It depends on the individual's needs, of course, but take a test that may give you an idea as to how ready you are. Take this situation that many of us find to be the most difficult for an author. It happens frequently. You meet someone, and in casual conversation you say that you've written a book. You're likely to hear, "Really? What's your book about?" Are you prepared to respond?

That's not public speaking, you may say. Maybe not the in the lectern-before-a-packed-hall sense, but to interest a casual acquaintance in your book in a mere sentence or two is quite a challenge.

How does that apply to you as a speaker? Speaking before a Kiwanis audience, you have only a few seconds in which to interest that collection of fidgety businessmen and women.

It works this way, too. Once, at a writers' conference, an agent asked an author to describe his book in 25 words or less. Two dozen words, plus one! After he had struggled uncountable hours on that manuscript, here was someone wanting him to reduce it to two sentences or less. He was so shocked by the request that he refused to do it, and, of course, the agent didn't offer to represent the writer's work.

Since then, we've thought about that requirement and decided that it wasn't such a mindless demand after all. The more you think about it, you may realize that it's what you say in answer to that unexpected question, and how you say it that determines whether or not you're a good salesman for your book. Having this skill may not be all that important for you as you prepare to sell your book in the friendly venues you'll select to open your bookselling campaign, but it will loom large when you turn to radio and television as media for selling your books.

Your audiences will expect you to speak well as a professional in the art of organizing words should, and they'll recognize it if you haven't done it well. Prepare yourself meticulously. Your experience in writing tells you that nothing clarifies your thoughts as much as writing them out and reviewing what you've written.

Write out your speech, especially if you're new at selling your books by speaking in public. Some of the best speakers do it. With a written speech, they can organize themselves, measure the time it takes to present it, and even choreograph their movements and the small gestures that make a successful speaker seem so spontaneous and natural. But do try to get away from the need to read your speech verbatim as soon as you can. A good transition from a written document to independence from notes is using 3"X5" cards with your speaking points written in a bullet format.

As a suggestion for your first presentation, you might think about writing notes to yourself in the margins. Your notes might include the names of people you want to recognize and thank publicly, reminders to leave your position behind the lectern (if there's room and if you have a microphone that'll allow you to move about) or even something general like, "Sell yourself." You may want a note that says, "Make eye contact." Thinking through and jotting down your thoughts like this will help you fit into the host's program and allow you some time to sell your book. You can still make the marginal notes, even if you use cards.

If you've never spoken in public at all, read your entire presentation aloud to test your voice and listen for awkwardness in construction or pronunciation. Some word selections register better being read silently than they do when read aloud. For example, if you were to use the word nuclear and unthinkingly pronounce it *nukelar* as is frequently done by prominent speakers who should know better, it could affect your listeners the same way as the sounds a beginner practicing on a bagpipe would.

For best results we suggest that you read it to a friend for feedback, or just to have the experience of speaking to a live audience, however small. Also, it's a good idea to purchase a small tape recorder to record your practices and the speeches themselves.

Before You Speak

Be sure that you and your hosts are in agreement on the basics of your presentation. Ask how long they will want you to speak. Will there be time for questions? And don't forget to help them present you. Have a biography prepared ahead of time and send it to whoever will introduce you. But bring another copy with you to the speaking event, just in case.

Even as you start selling your books by speaking in public, it's important to think of ways to increase the number of your listeners. At first, you may have to rely on the host organization to publicize your appearances. It's quite likely that they'll do that through their newsletter. Help yourself by offering to write a small piece about yourself and your book and ask them to insert it or send it to the local newspaper. This is a good time to think about coordinating an appearance on the local radio station with your speaking engagements.

If you're a person who doesn't handle well unexpected changes to the program, try to visit the room where you will speak. The host organization may have its own lectern with an amplification system. Most do, but if your voice is not strong enough to be heard by the hard-of-hearing in the back of the room, don't allow yourself to be caught short. You should ask for some amplification to be provided.

Always bring your books with you. Ask the host for a small table to display them before and during the event and where you can sit down after you speak to sign books and sell them.

Visuals can be extremely valuable in making your presentation more complete and effective, particularly if you are speaking after the meal and "just a short business meeting." If the event is a breakfast meeting, your listeners' minds are likely to begin wandering to their first business appointment of the day. At night, your problem may be to prevent them from falling asleep, but you'll still have to work at keeping them interested in you and your book. Having something for them to watch will help you retain their attention.

Depending on the type of visual aids you'll use, for instance, a PowerPoint presentation, you may find it worthwhile to arrive at your speaking venue early, if you can, to make yourself comfortable with the place and to be sure your equipment is set up to begin with a minimum of awkward delay. That may not always be possible, because these meetings are frequently held in restaurants or in rooms of buildings which may not be available until just before your listeners begin to arrive. Getting everything just the way you want it may prove to be impossible, but do try.

The more you can learn about the conditions under which you will speak, the better you can prepare yourself.

A final suggestion for your speaking preparations, one we've made earlier, is to remember to arrange some way to collect feedback from your audiences. You can always make notes based on your impressions or direct comments from your listeners. Have your small tape recorder handy for recording your presentation as well as your thoughts immediately after your event.

Be prepared to use your business cards, handouts, or a nicely-lettered sign at your book display. Whatever you do, be sure to leave each listener in your audience knowing your name, business address, as well as your e-mail address so that they can order books from you later.

You're On

If you have to read your speech to avoid embarrassing gaps or to keep from rambling, by all means do it, but as you improve and are relaxed as you begin to speak, strive to refer to your written material as little as possible. In fact, you may want to reduce your notes to a page with a few key ideas or words.

Personalize your opening. Refer to your host organization and to your connection with it. Greet people you know with a nod or by mentioning their names. Maybe you can mention a humorous exchange you have just shared with your host, but don't force it. If you're not good at jokes, don't tell them.

Follow your notes to move naturally and make hand gestures. And remember to make eye contact with the audience. Find friendly faces in the audience and speak to them. Watch how they respond to your humor or to your most profound points and speak to them.

And, of course, don't allow your remarks to slip very far from selling your book.

Afterward

Immediately after you speak, sell your books. That's primarily what you came to do, but a close second is to continue building an interest in your book. So, having done your best to create that interest, do your best to learn what they think. Talk to as many people as you can. This is the time to use that supply of cards that mention you, your book, and how to order it. Direct people to your website and ask for their comments.

Take the earliest opportunity to use your small tape recorder to document your impressions of how it went, the ideas that occurred to you, and the questions that were asked. Record also the comments you collected. As your presentations become more frequent, use a guest book at your table or some other means of collecting names and e-mail addresses so that you can send those people copies of your own newsletter if they have indicated an interest. Or just direct them to your website. You say you don't have a website? Get one. See Carl Loveland's informative discussion of websites in Chapter Thirteen.

Send notes thanking your host organization for the opportunity to speak to them. Robin and Linda Williams, nationally known Bluegrass performers, are particularly good at sending prompt, personalized, hand written notes thanking the producers of their performances. Let your audience know how to reach you.

Work to improve your presentation. Think about the questions you get. Use what you learn from your audiences to make your presentations even better.

Because our intention has been to write this book as a primer for authors with a single, recently published book, we make no claims that this chapter is a comprehensive treatment of the art of public speaking. Rather, it's intended to inform you of the benefits of a public speaking campaign to help you sell your book through your own efforts. We strongly suggest that you make full use of the vast store of resources available to help you become an effective public speaker.

Joe Sabah, a nationally known authority on the art of selling yourself and your book, has published a number of books. They're listed in our references pages. For practice and more suggestions we recommend you find one of the many groups organized to help their members become more effective speakers.

Radio Interviews

Earlier you read that one of your strategies as a public speaker is to maximize the scope of your audience. Everyone who hears you talk about yourself and your book is a potential buyer, and what better way to expand your market than by talking on the radio? It's a medium with many advantages over speaking before live audiences.

This is a great opportunity just because of the large number of listeners you can reach without ever having to leave your home. Another advantage is that the skills you've developed in speaking to live audiences translate very easily to the more anonymous but far broader medium of the radio interview.

Your local radio station can reach thousands of listeners, but if it is affiliated with a network, your potential exposure increases enormously. Not only that, but getting started is easier than you might think.

Getting Started In Radio

Use the Internet to find lists of radio stations across the country. This works for a local station as well as it does for one across the continent. You can derive a lot of information from the lists themselves about the programming offered by an individual radio station. You'll note that only a few may have interview programs in their listings, but don't be dissuaded. There are plenty of talk shows around, and most of the stations airing them have a website.

Go to the site of a station in an area you wish to target to find a telephone number for the program director for the talk show. Be ready to tell the director what you can talk about. Just be sure that your topic is relevant.

This shouldn't be a formidable challenge because if you've prepared yourself thoroughly to speak to the Chamber of Commerce, you should be ready to convince a program manager about what you can do to enhance a talk show. Don't be intimidated by making the call to someone who makes a living at radio broadcasting. You're a professional. Remember that talk shows have their own problems in filling their programs with speakers. Also, you can find plenty of help from experts in the field. For much more detail, we recommend Joe Sabah's book, *How to Get on Radio Talk Shows All Across America Without Leaving Home.*

Let's be honest, however. The larger the audience of the radio station you target, the larger will be the requirement that you and your book present a truly appealing message. The advice to start small is just as valid in radio as it is in testing your speech-making skills with small, friendly audiences.

Your Radio Message

The need to prepare for your first radio interview is just as important as it is in speaking to live audiences—if not more so—because with groups, it's your show and you the speaker control the message. In radio, it's the station's show and either the talk show host or the interviewer control the topics, the timing, and, most important, the leading questions.

Yes, of course you've read somewhere of a television interviewer who became famous by an incident of incisive questioning that forced a famous politician into a critical stumble. Keep in mind that it's almost always in the interest of the radio personalities to make themselves look good by conducting an interview that makes the guest look good.

Remember, too, that you can get over your initial apprehension by making your first broadcast appearances in a small, friendly setting. One of the authors of our book recalls her nervous feelings when she made her first radio appearance a few years ago:

"My woman's club group was invited to participate in a radio competition with other clubs in our area of the state. The event was sponsored by a big city newspaper, and we were asked to read all the newspapers for a specific week in preparation for the radio quiz.

"Five of us were asked to represent our club. We studied the papers, got together to quiz each other, then made our appearance.

"I remember having butterflies in my stomach as we awaited the opportunity to ring our bells as fast as possible before the competing team could ring theirs. Once the announcer began the event, adrenalin and all those hours of preparation took over. Even though my stomach churned, I answered those questions along with other of our team members and we won the competition.

"Years later, that nervous experience helped me in an appearance on NPR to advertise a conference for a branch of the National League of American Pen Women. That day we sat down in a small studio and answered questions asked by the program announcer.

"I was nervous and shaky, but my voice was steady and I remembered what to say. My experiences taught me that preparation is everything and being a little nervous is a good thing."

The experience you gained in preparing to speak to the Chamber of Commerce will apply to radio, but there are differences. In radio you don't warm up the audience according to a plan as you do with a live audience, so you'll have to prepare to be interesting from your first opportunity to speak. Instead of speaking to a group of people who are not likely to leave their seats until you're finished, in radio your challenge is to keep the interest of someone who may be listening to you while driving in the car, a person who has the entire radio dial to choose from. A dissatisfied radio listener can leave you just by touching the seek button.

Yet another significant difference is that many radio shows require that several speakers share the program time. Naturally, this has some significant effect on how you present yourself and your work. It could mean that you will have as much as a half-hour or less than ten minutes to tell your story. It may also mean that you are competing, in effect, with two other authors on the same program.

By listening to the programming of the show on which you'll appear, you can get a good idea of what kinds of questions to expect and how they will be asked, but still you must prepare for the unexpected. How will you respond if the interviewer poses a question this way, "In the twenty seconds remaining, would you tell our audience how you compare your protagonist with Tom Clancy's Jack Ryan?"

We recommend that you listen to interviews of prominent authors to hear how they handle questions and sell themselves. Terry

Gross, whose program *Fresh Air* is produced at WHYY in Philadelphia and broadcast nationally on the National Public Radio, is a good example. Her guests are personalities of the caliber of Pulitzer Prize winners and movie celebrities, so her guests are good examples of what to emulate.

On their website, the SBA Women's Business Center recommends intensive preparation for speaking in public just as we do. In their very informative website they recommend asking the producer or whoever is setting up the interview for some essential information prior to your appearance. These are things you'll want to know.

1. Is my book the topic of the interview, or simply a part of it? Why was it chosen?

2. Will the interviewer pull information from other sources to contrast to my story?

3. Will other authors be interviewed at the same time?

4. Does the interviewer want a list of suggested questions?

5. Will the interviewer want to see a synopsis of probable answers?

The Women's Business Center also makes recommendations for preparing your message.

1. Prepare and outline the specific points you wish to make.

2. Prepare concise opening and closing statements—they're often the most remembered statements you'll make.

3. Divide your message into sound bites and practice delivering them.

4. Outline your points and examples on notes or index cards and have them at hand.

5. Arrive at least 30 minutes early for interviews held at a studio.

You should arrange to meet the interviewer before the program and ask how you will address each other. Speaking on a first name basis is the best. This may be a good time to determine who will introduce your book and how much you will be permitted to talk about it.

But some things may be different if yours will be a telephone interview. Let's also look at some suggestions Joe Sabah provides on the Internet. In telephone interviews, just as in any speaking engagement, preparation is essential, but in some areas they are quite different from what you've done for a local event.

- Have a glass of water handy to lubricate the throat or to stifle coughs.
- Put a 25-foot cord on your telephone so you can stand while you talk. They're cheap and easily available.
- Familiarize yourself with the broadcast area covered by the station. If you use a state map, you might be able to sound like a native by mentioning place names.
- Another way to familiarize yourself with the station's local area is to listen to their weather and traffic.

And, of course, don't forget your manners. They apply just as much to radio interviews conducted from your kitchen table as they do with speaking to a live audience. Send a hand-written thank-you note and offer to appear again.

Publicists

A more formal, but generally expensive, way to market your book is through the use of a publicist. Publicists are professional marketing experts. Their role is to get you and your book known to the public. They charge a fee for their services based on the time, effort, and extent of those services, as well as on the benefit of their contacts and know-how.

Services Available

Publicists may use a variety of media avenues. They might prepare press releases or articles for the print media. They might set up events, such as book signings for you as well as the publicity for the events. They might arrange radio or TV interviews. They might put together a tour for you with a variety of media contacts in cities across the country.

Targeting Publicity

The publicist would need to identify where the market for your book exists in order to target the publicity. Who is the potential audience for your book? Would a national or regional campaign be cost effective? Does your book appeal to a specific segment of the public or to the general public? For instance, Sikes' book *Hotels to Remember* focuses on a number of exceptional hotels and the cities in which they can be found, appealing to a specific segment of the reading public, whereas a completely different segment of the population would be attracted to books for children.

Financial Realities

Publicists may charge by a time frame (hours, weeks) or by the type of service. For example, one publicist we contacted charges $1650 to set up ten radio interviews around the country, all conducted by phone. However, the typical cost of a package by an established publicist ranges from $3500 to $10,000 or more. It may be possible to find a smaller company that will provide specific targeted services for a fee under $1000. For example, to reduce the cost, the publicist might agree to offer consultative services such as recommending media contacts, providing a list of potential contacts, and perhaps reviewing your marketing plans.

Finding Publicists

We would suggest at least three areas to consider. First, try the Internet. Second, try area phonebooks. Third, talk with members of writers groups or others who may have knowledge of publicists in your region and get their recommendations. If your book is not self-published, your publisher may have access to publicists' services, so check them too. One of our authors found a publicist quite by accident when she read about her in an online e-zine.

You may want to consider acting as your own publicist, using some of the ideas contained in this book. It will take more time and effort on your part but will be less costly in cash outlay.

Whatever methods you use to promote your book—speaking about it in public, talking on the radio, promoting it through a publicist— you will learn and grow with each step you take. And with each new promotional technique you use, you, and your book, will become better known to the public.

You have created your own potent marketing package. You could be on your way to the bestseller's list!

CHAPTER EIGHT

How to Promote Your Romance Novel

by Mary Montague Sikes

Many people enjoy reading romance. According to Romance Writers of America, romance novels make up 48 per cent of all popular paperback fiction. That's a huge market. Each year these books produce over $1 billion in sales. Men as well as women can be counted among the readers of romance novels.

Because of the popularity of romance in the marketplace, authors often make the mistake of believing their books will be easy to promote. This is not necessarily true. Like other books, there will be a lot of _blood, sweat, and_ _tears_ involved in getting your romance book out and in demand.

If you are fortunate enough to have sold to Harlequin or Silhouette for one of their series lines, you will have the advantage of knowing your book will be on store shelves along side the books by other authors in that same line. For example, if your book is a Harlequin Intrigue, it will be on the shelf next to books by other Intrigue authors. If you are a new author, the disadvantage for you here is that readers often choose books by authors with whom they are familiar. Readers may buy most of the Intrigues out that month but possibly skip over yours because they have never heard of you. Your books will be on the shelf, but they may be ignored.

Another disadvantage for series books such as Harlequin and Silhouette is these books have a short bookstore shelf life—often only about three weeks. This is about the same life expectancy as a monthly magazine.

These same series books, however, may be available much longer through the publisher's website. They may be sold also through book clubs. These additional sales venues mean that writing for a Silhouette or Harlequin series line can bring in a good income for the author.

If you are published by a small publisher, you can expect your books to be available for a longer period of time. However, your books may not make it into the bookstores, and, if they do, they probably will not get a prominent location on the store's book shelves. Also, with small print runs, they will not have wide distribution to bookstores throughout the country.

Mid-list authors and authors with small publishers all face similar problems. These authors will need to learn how to market their own books.

Published! Now Sell It! has marketing ideas that will work for authors who must promote their own books. Here are some ideas that can help romance and other genre writers.

Book Signings with Another Author

My publisher for *Hearts Across Forever*, a romance, put me in touch with another one of her authors, Wendy Howell Mills, who wrote the mystery, *Callie & the Dealer & a Dog Named Jake*. Since, at the time, we lived in adjacent states and because Wendy's book cover is illustrated with my artwork, our publisher thought we might make a good book signing team.

We liked the idea, compiled a list of book stores, split it between us, and began making telephone calls. We were able to set up more than a dozen signings together in the Newport News, Hampton, and Richmond areas of Virginia over a period of several months.

Our first three book signings went very well. The next one was set for September 11, 2001. That signing, of course, was cancelled. Not only did the September 11 events put a damper on us personally, but the tragedy affected the book selling business as well. Fewer people were in the malls, and fewer people seemed inclined to buy. We went ahead, however, and rescheduled the signing for mid-October.

As Wendy and I grew more experienced with book signings, we found that it was nice and more effective to have someone with whom to share a book signing table. Most of the bookstores managers were considerate. Upon arrival they greeted us, helped us set up, and provided us with drinks and sometimes cookies.

Before we left each store, we signed our remaining books and attached to the front cover the "autographed copy" stickers they provided. When we did this, we were sure having autographed copies would help bring more book sales. Later, we were disappointed to learn that in many cases the signed copies were sent back to the publisher after only a short period of time had passed. Sometimes they kept the books only a few days or for as little as a week.

Lessons Learned at Book Signings

Here are some of the lessons we learned with these book signings:

1. An attractive poster illustrating your book will draw people to the signing table. The various Barnes & Noble stores made beautiful signs featuring the covers of our books. Employees placed these posters in prominent spots throughout their display areas and on outside windows. For other bookstores, we each brought our own Plexiglas stands with colorful signs to display on tables. After a few events, I had a color photograph of the two of us taken at

a book signing made into a display poster and printed at a commercial copier.

2. Bookmarks are good marketing tools. You can wander throughout the store and hand them out to interested customers. You may even try greeting customers at the door with a bookmark. Some stores like having bookmarks left at checkout areas for customers to pick up.

3. Having a niche helps. Wendy's book is set in the Outer Banks of North Carolina. Because many people in Virginia vacation there year after year, having a book set in that location generated extra interest in her book and created more sales. My book is set in Jamaica, but few people who came by our book signing tables in the Virginia bookstores had been to the island, so my setting did little to stimulate sales.

4. A bright tablecloth and fresh flowers enhance the signing area and attract buyers. While we did not have this as part of our book display, I noted the successful table setups of other authors and planned to use them in the future.

5. Location is everything. Having a setup near the front entrance to the store is a key to success. At one of the book signings that I did alone, my table was set up near a seldom-used exit door. Very few people ever saw my display.

6. Remember to be courteous. No matter how well or how poorly things have gone, be sure to thank those people who helped with the book signing. Thank you notes are important as well. Both Wendy and I sent thank you notes immediately following our events to the community relations manager or other person

who served as our host. Since I have note cards that feature my artwork from *Hotels to Remember,* I often leave a package of these as a small gift for my bookstore host.

Book Events Combined with Travel

When traveling out-of-state, I found it helpful to make contact a few weeks ahead of time with bookstores in areas where I planned to stay. On one trip I arranged signings in Savannah, Georgia, Hilton Head, South Carolina, and Jacksonville, Florida.

The Waldenbooks in Hilton Head Island is located in the community's attractive indoor mall. My table was at the store entrance and commanded a lot of attention, meaning that I sold all the books they had in stock.

Friends in Palm Springs, California helped set up a signing for me with a bookstore that was participating in the weekly Thursday evening Village Fest on Palm Canyon Drive. The event attracts a variety of artists, as well as clothing and food vendors and features live entertainment. Just being part of this street fair was fun, and it gave me ideas for future visits to Palm Springs.

On a trip to the island of Kauai, I contacted the major bookstores and set up signings before leaving home. I even sold books to people we met at a popular outdoor hamburger stand in one of the small waterfront communities. They loved having autographed and personalized copies of my romance novel.

Dress the Part

Romance authors often are invited to speak at conferences, for local writing or civic groups, and to book clubs. These are excellent opportunities for writers to promote and sell their books. These events are where image is especially important.

I admire writers such as *New York Times* bestselling author, Sherrilyn Kenyon who has developed an image she wants to project as the author of vampire books. She often wears black or dark-colored, flowing outfits that offset her long luxuriant red hair. Her memorable image is one that fans admire, and it sets her off from the crowd.

One writer I remember who presented a seminar at a conference a few years ago claimed she always put on a purple hat when she was writing. That alerted her family that she was doing business, so no one disturbed her. She wore that purple hat when presenting workshops and other programs.

Regency novelists enjoy dressing up in period costumes. They make a compelling image when they talk to groups or give conference workshops.

Writers of novels set in the west with cowboy heroes may wish to appear like the characters they create, so they sometimes wear leather, suede, and wide-brimmed hats. They are dressing the parts that go along with their book titles.

All of these styles of dress and many others stir up interest among readers and leave them with a memorable image of the author. However, some writers do not feel comfortable dressing up like the character from a novel. For these writers, the most important issue is to dress in a professional manner.

A few years ago, that often meant wearing a black suit, probably a pants suit, and a crisp white shirt or white sweater. Now women writers may feel more comfortable attired in a long floral dress or a suit with a bright colored shirt. The most important thing is for their choice of dress to be neat and well-fitted and for their shoes to be comfortable.

Other Things to Help Promote Sales

1. Always carry extra books in your car. You never know when books will fail to arrive at the store in time for your book signing. You also never know when you'll meet someone who wants to purchase your book.

When discussing my book with the owner of a restaurant where we often dine, I found he wanted to carry my books in his gift shop. Since I had a box of books in the car, I could accommodate his interest immediately while the idea was fresh in his mind.

2. Create a list of buzz words and phrases to help promote sales. For the romance writer, some of these might be: star-crossed lovers, brave hero, bold leader, defiant, majestic, dark brooding, rebel with a cause, strong upstanding leader, tortured past, headstrong heroine, and many others. Use your buzz words in short descriptions of the books you are promoting.

3. Make up a sentence to describe your book. For example:

Because of his love affair with a beautiful young student, the life of a philosophy professor takes a tragic turn.

An aging southern belle takes revenge after she spots her husband kissing another woman.

Having a brief description of your book memorized will help when the inevitable happens and someone asks you to tell what your book is about. You may want to have two different sentences in mind—one that centers around the romance and one that describes the mystery elements, if your book has them.

4. Create items that are connected to your book. You may want to sell these items or use them as giveaways. Bookmarks are good. I also have a line of note cards with artwork from *Hotels to Remember* on the front. These signed cards are carried in bookstores and gift shops in locations connected with the hotels highlighted in my book. While the hotels book is not a romance novel, I could make note cards from the art I created for the cover of my novel, *Hearts Across Forever.* If your image becomes popular, you may want to add to the line and include the image on coffee cups and other items. A word of caution—if you are not the artist who created the cover, you may need to get a signed release or permission from the creator of the artwork.

Writing Organizations Help Your Career and Your Sales

Some of the best advice I can give romance writers is to tell them to join Romance Writers of America, if they are not already members. I first learned about RWA a few years ago when a published member of the group spoke at a conference I was attending. Her talk left a lasting impression on me and on several other attendees as well. The organization sounded very professional, so I joined and have remained a member ever since.

The annual conference of RWA offers a variety of valuable benefits to writers, whether or not they are published. Not only does it give members the opportunity to meet other writers from all over the country and the world, but it also provides them the opportunity to attend workshops selected from more than 100 given by an outstanding array of professionals.

A conference handbook filled with valuable information sheets for most of the workshops is a priceless benefit of attending the annual event. In 1998 the Anaheim conference book held an amazing 470 pages of significant material. In 2002, the Denver handbook featured 202 pages.

Besides the handbook, the conference registration material includes a ticket for a visit to the "Goody Room" where thousands of free books, bookmarks, pens, pencils, tip sheets, and much more are given away. Conference attendees may promote their own books by contributing giveaway items for this room.

Major stars of romance such as Nora Roberts, Deborah Smith, Heather Graham, and many others attend these conferences, sign books, make talks, and mingle with other authors. Conference attendees can sign up for editor and agent appointments. For authors with published books who are looking for an agent, this is a good way to meet a variety of agents and possibly find one that might be right for you.

Besides networking, attending workshops, and seeing favorite authors, writers get the chance to attend meetings and workshops of affiliate chapters such as the Mystery-Suspense Chapter (Kiss of Death), the Regency Chapter (The Beau Monde), Faith, Hope, and Love, Inc., the Futuristic, Fantasy and Paranormal Chapter (FF&P), and the Gothic Romance Chapter. Most of these groups have active memberships with on-site events planned both before and after the conference. The affiliate chapters all have on-line list groups with hundreds of postings a day.

Other special interest chapters include: Chick Lit Writers, Celtic Hearts, Hearts Through History, Published Authors Special Interest Chapter (PASIC), On Line Chapter of RWA (From the Heart), RWA Online Homepage, Outreach International, and Electronic and Small Press Authors Network (ESPAN). Members of these chapters are supportive of their fellow writers and give advice and information that help them on the road to publication and book sales.

The final evening of the annual conference is devoted to RWA's version of the Academy Awards Oscar night. Members dress in lace and sequined gowns to attend the Rita and Golden Heart Awards events which in recent years have become theatrical productions. A lavish reception follows.

Future conference sites include: Atlanta, Dallas, San Francisco, Washington, D.C., Nashville, and New York City.

Many authors also promote their romance, mystery, paranormal, and other novels at the Romantic Times Booklovers Convention held annually. This is a fun, party time event with a giant book fair author signing that many writers look forward to attending each year.

Even when publishers work hard with their authors to promote books, it is still the author's responsibility to reinforce their efforts with promotion and publicity. Please refer to Chapter Four, Marketing with Visuals. The author's work on her own is part of the total marketing plan that one must have to succeed in the business of writing.

This plan should include working with the wholesale buyers. Many successful authors get to know these people, have meetings or lunch with them. In this way, authors widen their own knowledge of what works best to sell their books.

Let the wholesale buyer know if you have been interviewed for a newspaper article or a television segment. Let the buyer know about book signings you have scheduled.

Try to attend events where wholesalers may be speaking. Bring along your business cards, book covers, bookmarks, and flyers that you may wish to give these buyers.

For the author, promotion is an ongoing activity. Always be aware of opportunities, and always be ready to give your _blood, sweat, and tears_ to make your book an outstanding success.

"Art is a microscope which the artist fixes on the secrets of his soul, and shows to people these secrets which are common to all."

Leo Tolstoy, *Diaries*, May 17, 1896

CHAPTER NINE

Conducting Workshops

by Joseph Guion

An important method of promoting your artistic work is to provide workshops. Your expertise flows from the work you have performed in study, research, and practice. This basis for your workshops can provide additional marketing opportunities. It is essential that you consider using your book in the workshop. This demonstrates your expertise and provides an opportunity to show the book and its usefulness.

A workshop is basically a seminar or series of meetings for intensive study, work, discussion, and other activity. The term itself implies that attendees will not be passive, but will actively participate.

My book, *Love Songs on the Journey*, contains a series of poems and reflections on love of different kinds on one's journey to and with God. My expertise is not necessarily in poetry, but it stems from providing retreats and workshops for church leaders for twenty-two years. I have used my book in many of these efforts. Three important points are to select the proper parts of the book, the length of the passage used, and the places to use them. My leadership experience in the Navy, plus teaching leadership and management at the college level have added to this ability.

A workshop planning tool is at the end of this chapter, "A Workshop Outline Form," that I use extensively.

Workshop Preparations

My steps are similar to those in Chapter 4, Niche Marketing. The first step is to review and evaluate your expertise. Anyone who has written a book, painted or photographed published material, or taught subjects has developed expertise in the field. An important question is: "Would a workshop be more appropriate than a speech?" The purpose of your workshop will be to impart knowledge and skills to others *with their active participation*. Successful adult education and development are enhanced through the use of attendees' experience and participation.

The next step is to search for and select organizations and groups that might be interested in your workshop. The search should include civic organizations such as the Lion's Club, the Rotary Club and the Chamber of Commerce, which use guest speakers quite often.

There may be a natural connection between your capability and a market. For example, one of our contributors, Jean C. Keating, has written several books about dogs. She has a ready-made market with dog lovers and organized dog groups.

Others may not have such an easy connection. *Love Songs on the Journey* is religious in nature, but there are other markets that flow from the book. Since part of the book relates to caregivers and those who have lost loved ones, religious groups, caregivers, and grieving persons might be interested in workshops.

The steps for selecting the text include: 1. looking for a natural fit to choose the particular text with the best place in the presentation, 2. meeting the needs of the participants, 3. selecting unique or telling points reinforced by the book.

My poems are in a two-column format per page. Most of the poems are one or two columns, while several cover two pages—too long to read, unless the gathering is a poetry workshop. There are pages of "Pit Stops," with very short poems, ranging from one verse to four or five. I read one or two quite often.

One Pit Stop is "Today."

> God,
> Help me
> To love more today,
> It's the only day
> I have.

The choice depends on what the writer wants to do with the material. I use many of the book's poems and reflections in retreats and workshops for motivational purposes and to make a point.

An important decision in preparing for the book's use is to decide whether to use the book itself or to take excerpts from it. Unless the presentation follows the order of the book material, it is more difficult to use the book itself. Marking passages and moving from presentation to the book and vice versa brings challenges. It is too easy to miss a section in the book or to use something out of order. Cutting out pages of the book and inserting them in the presentation pages can make the book seem of little value. Excerpts can be used as handouts or as visual aids.

Whatever method you choose, you must practice enough so that the transition from presentation to book to presentation is smooth and not distracting. If your choice of how to use the material does not work well, change the method.

Contacting the Market

The first contact you make with a group requires an approach that demonstrates your enthusiasm and knowledge of the workshop subject matter. Talk about advantages and applications for that market. Find out what the group is seeking, and you may be able to adjust your approach to fit their needs.

You need advance information to tailor your workshop to best meet the group's needs. Gather information, such as demographics, gender make-up and perhaps age range, and try to learn about the history and experience of the people. A few groups have touchy subjects that they may want to avoid. Other groups may want you to address those subjects in order to resolve them. Try to fit the workshop to the groups' needs, not your own.

Before providing the workshop, try to attend a regular meeting of the group to view their dynamics and learn more about the people and how they react to each other. This is very important in a team-building workshop.

Small Groups

I use small groups in my teaching as well as in retreats and workshops. Certain workshop needs require small groups, particularly when different ideas are important and when one of the goals is to develop unity of purpose.

Small groups are essential in learning to work together. Four stages of group formation are noted:

1. <u>Storming</u> – the group flails around with little or no progress, not knowing how to start, who is in charge, how they will work together, etc. Emotional responses impede progress.

2. <u>Forming</u> – the group begins to settle down, individuals adjust to roles in the groups, a task leader emerges or is selected, and a support leader emerges who helps to build and maintain relationships.

3. <u>Norming</u> – the group develops norms of behavior, methods of making decisions, and begins to set goals or the direction in which the group will move.

4. <u>Performing</u> – the group is set and works together to accomplish its goals and complete its tasks.

There is no set time frame for these stages to occur. Team building activity shortens the length of time to the performing stage. Whenever I invite people to share, I remind everyone that we respect another's silence and that we do not require all participants to speak.

Facilitating Groups

Facilitating groups may require different approaches and skills suited for the group. Handling open discussions with a large group often requires the facilitator to be more active. The facilitator needs to stop a discussion periodically to summarize key points, otherwise the direction of the discussion can get lost. Sometimes the facilitator needs to gently, sometimes firmly, get the participants back on the subject. A participant may keep talking about a subject until it is "beaten to death." Another may bring up a personal agenda that has no bearing on the content.

Sometimes a participant talks too much so that others cannot get involved. When the facilitator walks toward that person, the "offender" often quiets down, perhaps because the facilitator's physical presence has expanded. When you stand over a seated person, your dominant position increases your power without changing the tone of the discussion. You may ask the talker to set his point aside for later discussion. If nothing else works, call a five-minute break and speak to the person privately.

Types of Workshops

Workshops can be found in professional, religious, and other fields. For example, one focuses on Architectural Design while others cover many of the Building Trades. Visual arts include drawing, painting, and photography. In theater you can include drama, acting, dance, stage activity, and playwriting. Most of my work is in the area of religious retreats and workshops. I am not including retreats here because they concern a specific religious denomination. Please review the chapters in this book to see possibilities in fields like your own.

This chapter concentrates on two workshops that I am most familiar with, Team Building and Caregivers.

Team Building

Team building is important in most human endeavors. Few people live and act alone. In formal and informal groups the ability to work together is the key to success. Factors that are important in developing a good team include: Trust, Respect, Open Communications, and Unity of Purpose. It takes time to develop these goals, so that a team or group can function well.

Nine years of building teams at the college level and twenty-some years in helping parish leadership taught me that the first step is to get people to relax in an informal setting. This step includes a demonstration of non-threatening activities that encourage people to share a brief life experience. Often a contact person will assure me that members of the group know each other. Most of the time they do not know each other well, so I use ice-breakers and methods of sharing non-threatening subjects.

Early in the workshop I usually tell a story or read a specific poem about my own mistakes, to show participants that we all have failures. My story or poem encourages participants to open up during the workshop to acknowledge and discuss human frailties, thereby building trust and respect for each person. In parishes, I sometimes use the image of a car on a handout and a listing of a car's major parts. Participants mark the list in answering the question, "What part of the car are you?" This effort never fails to bring out humor and informality very quickly.

Sharing good experiences work well initially because people are more apt to share their successes than failures. As the workshop progresses deeper sharing develops. This enables people to speak openly even though they have differences of opinion. Although some participants get edgy and want "progress," time devoted to sharing and discussion helps in working together to reach selected goals.

Caregivers

A Caregivers Workshop is devoted to helping people in stressful situations to take needed time out for themselves and to provide an opportunity to learn ways of coping with their situation. A key point is to help participants feel free to open up and tell their story. In telling of their experience, they find that others have the same fears, anger, denial and guilt.

The beginnings of these workshops are similar to team building, except that the emphasis is on encouraging and allowing the caregivers to have more time to feel free to speak and share. Although it may seem like the people are wasting time, "wasting time together" is an important step to free people up to speak. The subject matter is often quite emotional, so the feelings of the attendees must be carefully considered.

I often use a poem "The Love Triangle," to include God in a family or spousal love relationship between the caregiver and the patient. The point that God is love is in my religious tradition and in The Bible.

The leader assumes that the persons attending a Caregivers Workshop do not know each other. The atmosphere in the workshop has to be informal, relaxed, and open. The first step is the same as other workshops, getting people to know something about each other to encourage them to speak freely. This is done best in small groups. Some are reluctant to talk about their experiences. Helping the participants take time to get acquainted encourages more and more openness. Giving people time to talk about a subject helps to encourage more sharing.

My caregiving experience helps in breaking down barriers of silence and reluctance. I freely speak of my successes and failures as a primary caregiver for my late wife. You, the leader, need to share the story first. Telling your story encourages the participants to share their own. Allow people to drag out their stories if needed. The purpose of this workshop is not to get something done, but to free people to speak of their experiences.

Many "experts" believe that men do not share their feelings. In two recent men's retreats I was amazed once again that people want and need to share their feelings, but they need the proper time, place and atmosphere. The main idea is to make sure that the environment is non-threatening. Much of that stems from the facilitator's manner and freedom to share failures and successes. Your efforts to listen in a non-judgmental way encourage others to do the same. I use the poem, "I'm Glad," which tells about my attempts to please my wife during our fifty-year marriage. It encourages participants to do the same.

A surprise result of that poem stemmed from the wife of one of the men participants. She said that her husband came home from the retreat and kept saying, "I love you," most of the day until she got tired of hearing it. We should all hear that phrase too often.

Session Planning

Preparing your workshop sessions consists of organizing the subject matter and skills needed in a logical movement to a conclusion. Please see the planning tool at the end of this chapter. Writing out the purpose of the workshop and the goals to be accomplished should be first. List the materials, equipment and visual and other aids you will use. Set up a step-by-step process to accomplish your goals. Have motivational material, examples, and anecdotes ready for use at any time when you see attention and participation lagging.

A good motivational example that attracted immediate attention and set the tone of a presentation occurred in the Navy Instructor's School when I was the Officer-in-Charge. A fledgling instructor selected a session where he would teach young sailors about automobile safety. This would be a boring subject for young people who believe that they will live forever.

The instructor-trainee brought in a bucket containing a large ball of wet newspaper. He slammed the ball against the chalkboard and said quietly, "That's your head hitting the windshield at sixty miles an hour." The sailors knew immediately that the water dripping down the board represented their blood.

The dramatic action in the example is not the only way to begin a motivational piece. Using the book's material is a good motivational tool and also helps to make it easier for sales. The use of the book's material should be explained early in the first session. One reason for doing this is to alert the participants to listen for ideas that they might glean from the book. It is a good idea to show why it is logical to use the book for motivational and informational purposes.

Leading questions can bring attention to your subject matter. Presenting little known facts and ideas, especially from the book, can motivate participants to get interested.

The Workshop

Introduction

The workshop should begin with an introduction that contains motivational material. You cannot assume that all the material you present will keep people on the edge of their seats. Motivational material can be "ice breakers," anecdotes or other stories, and vivid visuals. Provide a brief outline of your workshop very early. Invite questions and responses from participants to determine if they are satisfied with what you will cover. They may have different desires and expectations.

Your enthusiasm for the subject goes a long way toward generating enthusiasm among participants. Set the tone of your workshop through the initial environment, your appearance and manner. I use music and art to create an atmosphere of relaxation and informality. An informal approach works best when you desire to get people to loosen up and participate.

Visual aids are extremely important. They range from professional projection equipment to the use of an easel and handouts. You have to present points visually one at a time or participants will move ahead of you in scanning the aid. Cover up parts of the visual until you come to the next point. Do not give a handout until you have introduced it or presented the information or you lose eye contact and attention. Please do not read visuals to adults unless they cannot see the text or pictures clearly.

Sessions

Set up sessions to provide about an hour of material including initial sessions that help participants to know each other and to share. Other sessions include information and practical application separated into two or three major points.

For example – Point One

The presentation begins with a statement of the point followed by motivation, such as examples, questions, and anecdotes. A short segment from the book would probably be very useful here.

If a skill of some kind is being taught, it is broken down into easy steps so that participants have time to absorb the information and to practice the skill. As participants go through their efforts, make suggestions and ask questions to be sure that they know what to do. Be kind to slower ones and give them assistance so that the group can go forward to the next step together. If a participant is quick and accurate, he or she might help to bring the slower person along. Wrap up the first point with a brief summary.

Make sure that you give participants a break between sessions. This time helps to keep people alert. It gives them time to share ideas and to surface questions.

Be careful about using too much of the book. It will seem that the only reason for the workshop is to sell the book. If it seems that interest is lagging or if the workshop gets too serious, it might be a good idea to bring some humor into the presentation. I have used "A Wake-up Call," which describes the first sight of a sleepy person's reflection in the mirror. It usually gets some laughs. The punch line at the end has a message, "God loves that face!"

Points two and three follow the same process in the session. It is important that the sessions build to a higher level of information, interest, and participation.

Summary

The summary is a mirror image of the introduction's main points without the need for additional motivation. Move briefly and rapidly through the information and activities to be sure that participants accomplish the goals for the session.

Near the end, point out features of the book and suggest they look at the book before they depart. Use a choice point or a favorite quote from the book to reinforce the desire for people to take a look at the book. A unique or humorous point is a good way to end a session.

Have fun doing your thing, and attendees will too. Your enthusiasm and motivating efforts will carry you through some difficult times. Make yourself available for questions and sharing ideas afterward. If you've done well, you will be asked to bring your expertise to another group.

Since your workshop will be related to the topic of your book, you need a sufficient number of copies available for purchase by participants. In some cases, you may wish to have the cost of a copy of your book included in the price of the workshop.

A WORKSHOP OUTLINE FORM

Primary Purpose: To impart knowledge and/or skills

Secondary Purpose: To develop unity and commitment

Goals:
>
> To have attendees understand information and/or accomplish skills.
>
> To develop community and relationships (For teamwork and situations where people need to work together.)
>
> To develop commitment (if needed).

MATERIALS: easel and writing pad, markers, handouts, visual aids, tape recorder, tapes, etc.

Start Time
Emphasis
End Time

INTRODUCTION
SESSION 1
>
> PRESENTATION
> RELATED SKILLS
> END PRESENTATION

BREAK
SESSION 2
>
> PRESENTATION
> RELATED SKILLS
> END PRESENTATION

BREAK

SESSION 3 (IF NEEDED)
    PRESENTATION
    RELATED SKILLS
    END PRESENTATION

SUMMARY

Note: If the workshop continues for more than a three-hour period, the sessions continue as above with a final wrap up.

"Language is the dress of thought."

Samuel Johnson, *Lives of the English Poets*

CHAPTER TEN

Using Photography to Promote Your Book

by Mary Montague Sikes

Let your own artistic talents tell about your book. Using your art and photographic skills to promote yourself will save you time and money.

Conventional or Digital Camera?

For years, I have carried my 35mm SLR Minolta Maxxum 7000 camera on every business or vacation trip I've taken. Having the camera with me meant that I could snap multiple pictures of places and events and keep them for future reference. It also meant that I had to buy dozens of slide projector carousels to file and store the many thousands of color slides in my collection.

Now I have a small digital camera that takes amazing photographs. Even using the five mega-pixel setting, I can store hundreds of clear images on a small space inside my computer.

The Minolta has been set aside for special occasions, such as weddings or other events that may require more depth in the image than the digital camera provides. Because it has an excellent wide-angle lens, I use the Minolta when an unusual need arises. One such need is photographing my work on display inside an art gallery. A trip to a new location that will present many picture-taking opportunities also may inspire me to haul around the much heavier 35mm SLR.

With the Minolta, I have the added concern of getting film through security at airports. Although the agents assure travelers that unless their film is a very fast speed (such as 1000 ASA) the screening equipment will not damage it, I know that is not necessarily true. When you have several airplane changes during your trip, you may go through security many different times. All those extra x-ray scans can cloud your unused film and damage the film that already holds your latest prize shots.

You can purchase a special lead-lined bag to protect your film. However, when my carryon luggage is scanned with the protective bag inside, it is always pulled off for a hand search. Apparently, the lead bag leaves a void inside the luggage visible on the scanner screen that triggers suspicion, so you might as well take out your film and request a hand search to begin with.

Take Pictures Wherever You Go

Once I arrive at my destination, I spend a lot of time looking for scenes that I may want to use in the future, then I photograph them. I always am looking for unusual angles and dramatic lighting. When I return home, I file my new slides in a 140-slot carousel and label it with the date and location of my trip.

Several years ago, I sent an art media kit, along with my writing media kit, to my book publisher. The art media kit related to the coffee table book on which the publisher and I were working at the time. She put the art folder aside, and I forgot that I had sent it.

Later, when she was looking for artwork to appear on covers for two of her books, she remembered my art folder. When she looked through it, she found a striking photograph I had taken in early evening light while walking near a wide, sandy beach along the Atlantic Ocean.

The picture shows a man walking his dog by the water's edge. Because my publisher needed a cover that featured a similar subject for a book set in the Outer Banks of North Carolina, she offered me a contract for use of my photograph. The picture turned into the cover art for *Callie & the Dealer & a Dog Named Jake* by Wendy Howell Mills.

Another picture—this one of my large painting of iris—became the cover art for a mystery novel centering on a piece of artwork by Georgia O'Keeffe. That book is *Affinity for Murder* by Anne White.

Cover art by Mary Montague Sikes
The original cover is in color.

This is an example of why it is important to take photographs and keep a file of them.

My artwork also was used for the cover of another of my publisher's books, *Red Room Rendezvous* by Paulette Crain. Portions of my paintings from photographs I took form the covers of my novel *Hearts Across Forever* and my coffee table book *Hotels to Remember.*

Using a Scanner

By the time I needed photographs to publicize and promote my books, I already had a large number stored on my computer. Those that were not stored could be scanned in my Visioneer 5550 when I needed them. Even my 35mm color slides could be scanned and used. The ever-evolving technology has proven to be a huge help to those producing promotional materials.

It only takes a little "know how" with the digital camera and space on your computer to make folders for picture files. Later, if you need the room, you can burn copies of your pictures on disks. Disks require less storage space than photographs or slides.

Photographs from the digital camera are loaded directly into the computer. This saves the time needed to scan regular photographic prints.

Choosing the Right Digital Camera

When we decided that it was time to purchase a digital camera, my husband spent many hours investigating the many varieties of cameras on the market. We eventually selected a Sony Cyber-shot because we liked the large LCD screen on the camera for viewing photographs.

Because I can easily view on the screen each shot taken, the camera's delete feature is made easier to use. After shooting a group of pictures, while still on site I go back through them and delete any that are not acceptable. That frees up space on the memory stick, so I can take additional shots if I need them.

Since I use the camera in my freelance photography work, I have found the feature of setting the camera for the five mega-pixel image size to be extremely helpful. My camera goes from 5M down to a small e-mail size. In-between settings include 3.2M, 3M, and 1M.

Because the size of the picture can be reduced from the 36 by 27 inches of the 5M shot, I always leave my setting on 5M. That way I have the highest quality photograph available for my use. You can always downsize your high quality image, but you cannot enlarge a low-resolution digital photograph.

We purchased a 256-megabyte memory stick for the Sony digital camera. A 32-megabyte memory stick came with the camera, but when using the 5M setting the smaller memory stick does not hold enough images to meet my needs.

Using Photos with News Releases

Whenever I want to include a photograph with a news release, it is simple to go into the My Pictures folder on my computer and pick an appropriate shot. For example, when Jean C.

Keating and I were scheduled to present a program about *Published! Now Sell It!* for a writer's symposium, I went to My Pictures and selected a photo that included Jean and me.

Next, I cropped and reduced the picture to a smaller image size suitable to send over the Internet as a JPEG. Then, I went to my address book and decided which newspapers might be interested in carrying a story about the talk we were scheduled to make. The photo was attached to e-mails sent out to each of the chosen newspapers. Most of the papers published the photograph as well as the story.

Just be sure the newspapers to which you send your photos and articles will accept e-mail attachments. Some do not.

Always Carry Your Camera with You

Always take your camera with you. With the digital, you have a camera that will easily slip into a pocket or purse. I have a sporty-looking little bag that holds the camera, an extra set of rechargeable batteries, battery charger (in case I need it), my spare memory stick, and the book of instructions that came with the camera. The bag is large enough to also carry a small purse and other personal items. It is perfect to use as my handbag for trips I take by air.

Photographing Artwork

For those of you who want to photograph your art as well as take pictures to promote your book, you will need to assemble a few items and have them ready for a photo session. I keep two large pieces of black burlap in my studio closet. When the need arises, I am ready to pull the cloth out, attach it to the studio wall with pushpins, and then hang my work on nails tacked into the fiber wall covering.

During the daylight hours, I normally do not need extra illumination. The studio has three large skylights that flood the wall with natural light.

In the studio closet, I keep a heavy-duty metal tripod with sturdy legs that can be adjusted up and down. My Minolta SLR screws into the tripod. I also have a shutter release cable that I can attach to my tripod-mounted camera. With this setup, I can count on a steady camera whenever I need to take pictures.

The film I use is Kodachrome 64 for slides. Slide film is becoming harder to find and is no longer found in stores such as Wal-Mart. Most of the time slide film is available in camera shops.

The artwork is placed horizontally on the black burlap. Then I position the tripod so the camera is focused directly in the center of the work. I turn my lens adjustment to the 50-mm setting and take at least six or eight shots of each piece of art.

Since I like having quick access to my photos, I also take several shots of each painting with the digital camera. As soon as I finish taking the digital pictures, they can be put directly into the computer. The digital shots can be used for many purposes, including note cards, websites, promotional prints, bookmarks, and more.

It is important to drop the slide film off for processing at a camera shop. Do not use a drug or discount store's one-hour photo labs if you wish quality results. Unless the chemicals are fresh, you will be disappointed in the photographs and will complain about their lack of quality.

Most camera shops will need to send the Kodachrome slide film away for processing. Usually that will take about a week, so you will need to plan on the extra time if you are counting on pictures for a special promotional project.

In conclusion, choose the camera equipment that is right for you, and remember to carry it with you wherever you go. Use your scanner and digital camera programs to make the most of your creative skills. Your artistic abilities combined with your knowledge of words can bring joy to your work.

Make a list of all the creative ways you can use your photographs to promote yourself and your work. Then, tape the list near your computer and refer to it often. Being able to illustrate your writing with photographs will enrich your life as a writer.

"Writing is nothing more than a guided dream."

Jorge Luis Borges, *Dr. Brodie's Report*, Preface

CHAPTER ELEVEN

Making the Most of Television Appearances

by Mary Montague Sikes

Your first television appearance can be an intimidating experience that makes you wonder if the rewards are worth the tension. However, even though the cameras make you nervous, take a deep breath and consider the benefits. After all, from small segments on local channels to national TV interviews, television is an outstanding way to make your work known as a writer or as an artist.

My first television experience came a few years ago when I was part of a collaborative art project. Six artists were involved in the joint effort. Each of us had the responsibility for making a video tape in which we introduced ourselves and described our individual artwork for the project. Then all six tapes were combined into one tape, copies of which were sent to the media. This television tape played a major role in the selection of our project as part of a national conference held in a major city where we received considerable press coverage.

That one example of the value of television as a marketing tool for creative people made a lasting impression on me. Now I take special notice of others, especially writers and artists, who use television opportunities to their advantage.

How to Get on Television

Ginger Levit, a fine arts and media consultant, is one of those people I have admired over the years. She has had 10 years experience in radio with Virginia News Network and Virginia National Public Radio and has made television appearances as well. An astute observer of television personalities, Levit points out that she pays careful attention to their mannerisms and how they dress for their TV appearances. She has favorites that she likes to emulate when she has an opportunity.

"First of all, you must have a worthy product or project to present," Levit says, "and you must have the confidence to speak about it knowledgeably."

She advises authors who are promoting books to "get a good grasp of the subject" so they can speak with authority. "Knowledge of a subject breeds confidence and the ability to speak smoothly."

Levit points out that the author or artist seeking a television spot needs to do some homework to find out who sets up the programming. In most instances that will be the public affairs coordinator for the radio or television station. The author then should call that person to make a pitch.

To prevent a case of sudden nerves, the author needs to write out the important points about the book promotion and offer good reasons for being accepted as a television guest. Should the author reach an answering machine, he or she must be prepared to leave a concise message with a contact telephone number. If after a day or two there is no response, the author should follow up with another telephone call. More often than not, persistence pays.

Another option for the writer or artist is to send out a press release addressed to the proper person. When a press release is used to seek a TV appearance, the author needs to follow up with a telephone call.

What to Do Before the Camera

Levit says that most television spots will run three to five minutes. "Organize the talk so you can speak without looking at notes," she advises. "Make good eye contact with the camera."

How you look into the camera is especially important, Levit explains. "Always look straight into the camera unless talking to somebody, such as in an interview. Then try to achieve balance between eye contact with the guest and with the camera," she adds.

"Basically pretend that the lens of the camera is somebody's eyes and look directly into it to command the attention of the unseen audience," Levit says. "This makes you look thoughtful and sincere."

What to Wear

On-camera clothing is important for both men and women. Often, television anchors create an image for themselves by the way they dress. Certain CNN personalities regularly wear casual clothing. Those on assignment in Iraq or some of the Hollywood lifestyle commentators who have developed their own ways of dress are examples.

Sportscasters often wear casual clothing, and that is what the viewer expects. The women anchors on one national network have their own personal characteristic dress style. One enjoys wearing short skirts and pastel colors; another almost always wears a pantsuit.

Take care when selecting clothing and jewelry for television appearances, Levit advises. For women she suggests a v-neck top with no jewelry "unless one has an extremely long neck." In that case, she advises a scarf tied around the neck or a turtleneck.

At one time necklaces were a "no-no," Levit says. "Women are wearing pretty necklaces more and more now," she points out.

For her own television appearances, Levit says, "I dress the way I always dress and wear jewelry. I have two or three classic pieces that I wear all the time."

Levit notes that care should be taken when wearing eye shadow for television appearances. Some eye shadow is needed, she says. It should be blended from not too dark on the eyelid to a very light tone above the lid.

"Not blending, especially blues, greens, and mauves, comes up on the screen as having created a garish thick line that looks artificial," Levit says.

For the eyebrow, she prefers feathery strokes that blend and darken without creating an artificial look. She cautions against using long thin lines on the eyebrow.

Choice of color for a television outfit also is important. "White is extremely flattering to brunettes," she observes. "Color also can be very flattering, such as hot pink, red, or turquoise."

For men, Levit likes a pale blue shirt with a tie. "Dress in a way to command respect," she advises.

One of Levit's most important tips for getting a spot on television is for the author or artist to offer to give a portion of the proceeds from his or her work to a non-profit organization. Television stations like to promote good causes, and this can lead to spots on a noon news show, she points out. It also can give the author or artist access to the organization's mailing lists.

Taped for Television

Sylvia Hoehns Wright, an environmental lobbyist and eco-savvy landscape gardener, has considerable experience with appearances in front of the television camera. She has done five-minute "stand alone" segments as well as a 30-minute feature.

For Wright's appearance on the PBS show, *VA Home Grown,* the show's host and his crew visited her woodland gardens. There, they filmed areas of the property while Wright and the host talked. Eventually, the cameras turned on her, Wright says. Later, three hours of filming at her garden site were cut to make a 15-minute television segment.

Wright was asked to wait in the greenroom as the garden part aired. "A few minutes before the segment ended, I walked onto the stage and the cameras focused on me and the host," she recalls. "For the next 10 minutes, we talked on live TV."

Her television appearance ended with five minutes of questions called in from the audience. "This opportunity provided the experience of multiple media activities," Wright says.

Because she often speaks in public, Wright found it easy to maintain her poise as she interacted with the host. The fact that the two of them talked at length the day her gardens were filmed also helped put Wright at ease for her on-camera live appearance.

On another occasion, she took part in a 30-minute panel discussion of environmental issues on live TV in Richmond. "I'm not sure we always faced the cameras," Wright says, "but at least the viewing audience saw a candid real-life discussion of diverse opinions."

Live Television Is Like Speaking in Public

Wright emphasizes that being on live television is similar to speaking before groups. The difference is that television reaches audiences that range from thousands to millions of people.

"All the rules that apply to effective speaking apply before a TV audience," she states. "You want to look the part—have a well-put-together and appropriate professional image. You need to speak clearly and use a vocabulary that fits your audience."

Nervous habits such as playing with one's hair or moving hands to make a point can be distracting and should be avoided. Wright finds repetition of words such as "okay" to be disruptive as well.

"Most of all, truly listen to the host's questions," she advises. "There is nothing wrong with clarifying a question or stalling for a second to format your thoughts before you open your mouth.

"With live TV, there is no opportunity to edit. What you say is what is heard."

As with radio or press interviews, it is always a good idea to offer a suggested list of questions ahead of time and hope that the host will use them. Sometimes authors get unexpected questions about the income they make on their books. It is a good idea to have a response ready for that type of inappropriate question.

Wright has appeared on local television stations in five-minute features where she discussed or demonstrated gardening activities. In these instances, the TV anchor coached her for a few minutes prior to broadcast.

"To be effective, you need to be aware of the differences in lighting, set up, and camera position," Wright recalls from the coaching sessions. "Being aware of stage requirements enables you to appear more comfortable and natural."

Learn to Use Television as a Promotional Tool

Because television is so important in today's society, writers who feel confident in their products—their books—should make an effort to pursue TV appearances wherever possible. Those authors who get on television can expect to see an increase in the popularity for their books. If they make a good impression, they also can expect to find themselves in greater demand as radio or club speakers.

If the thought of a television appearance puts butterflies in your stomach, try taking a deep breath, closing your eyes, and imagining you are making your first television appearance. Watch your favorite television hosts and follow their on-screen examples. Begin small by approaching the community channels that reach limited audiences.

If your first appearance is not what you hoped or planned, don't despair. Keep working to create the television image you want. Then follow your marketing plan to success.

Don't give up. If you make your books or art known to the public, the results will be well worth the effort.

"How many a man has dated a new era in
his life from the reading of a book."

Henry David Thoreau, *Walden*

CHAPTER TWELVE

Utilizing E-mail, Internet, and Newsletters

by Mary Montague Sikes

Having the world at their fingertips has changed the way writers work. No more pounding away at a manual typewriter, nor even an electric one. With continuing advancement in the field of computers, the writer can accomplish much more in far less time than anyone dreamed possible only a few short years ago.

Handling E-mail

Today, how writers use the Internet often deals as much with their organizational skills as with anything else. You as a writer will need to plan your day to include enough computer time to handle an onslaught of incoming e-mail. The amount of e-mail you receive will be especially heavy if you belong to several writers' groups or other organizations that keep messages flowing.

Many writers' associations have e-mail group lists to which members may belong. Romance Writers of America (RWA) has several lists connected with it as well as a number of sub-groups for genres that include paranormal romance, gothic romance, and mystery-suspense writers. There are state organizations such as Virginia Writer's Club and Virginia Romance Writers. Both of these groups have active e-mail loops.

Writers who belong to this many groups and who have other personal internet contacts as well are likely to receive 200 e-mails or more each day. It's easy to see how people with varied interests may find themselves deluged with a multitude of e-mails they want to read but may not have time.

Virus-Blockers, Firewalls, and More

Unfortunately, you cannot always trust what comes to you from the Internet. To keep your computer from receiving unwanted messages, you will need to have a spyware checker such as AdAware SE or Spybot, which are free on the Internet and a firewall such as ZoneAlarm, which is also free for non-commercial use. These will remove some of the unwanted e-mail but not all of it.

To further protect your computer, you will need to select a virus-blocker. Some e-mail providers are furnishing them free to their customers. A freeware virus scanner is available at http://free.grisoft.com/freeweb.php/doc/2/. You may want to purchase McAfee or Zone Alarm with a virus checker. These update daily and may be money well-spent.

You will need to scan through message titles, delete those not worth your time, then read through the ones that have meaning for you. Often, you will learn important news about publishers, agents, new book lines, and much more from e-mail messages. In fact, you will know about the book industry's business moves long before magazine updates have time to arrive in the mail.

To make the most of e-mail potential, you need to participate by contributing to discussions, especially those that deal with the publishing industry. As you send messages to your groups and to your friends, you can promote your new book with a line in your e-mail signature that shows up each time you send a message.

For example:
Mary Good Writer
www.marygoodwriter.com
My Life Story, Good Writer Press

One popular writers group internet list has designated a special day each week when it is acceptable to send out promo letters to that list. On promo day, the list is filled with e-mails identified with "promo" written in the subject line. The author then includes information about forthcoming book releases with a short blurb about the book. Authors may send out information about book signings, websites, contests, what readers are saying about their books, and much more.

Newsletters

Sometimes, authors who put newsletters on their websites will announce that a new newsletter has been posted and will give the link. They may go on to list the contents of that newsletter, and, if several other authors have contributed, those names will be listed. Often an author will interview another writer and feature that article in the newsletter.

Using e-mail is a great way to exploit the power of newsletters, which are an important promotional tool. From your internet groups, you can build a list of those who would like to receive e-mail copies of the newsletter. Or you can simply place the newsletter on your site and send out e-mails letting people know a new newsletter has been posted.

Whether your newsletter focuses on romance, travel, suspense, gothic, or another genre, you may wish to ask your writer friends to contribute articles for it. This arrangement will be a win-win situation. You will have a bigger newsletter. Your friends will have extra exposure and may even gain their own following of readers.

For most groups, the days of mailed newsletters are dwindling. Newsletters are sent as e-mail attachments, or, as mentioned earlier, members are alerted to go to the group website to read it. This saves money on postage and helps pay for the website.

The mystery/suspense chapter of RWA publishes a bi-monthly newsletter crammed with useful information for writers. It is available on the organization's website, where members may read it or print it out for reference. A notice is included in the newsletter that gives permission for other RWA chapters to reprint material if the author and the newsletter both are credited.

When your book is released, draft a letter that briefly describes your story and send it to your e-mail friends. Ask them for their reaction to your letter, and, if you get a positive response, send it to other e-mail lists to which you belong.

Using the Internet for Research

These days almost anything you want can be found on the Internet. If you are researching a topic, just put the word out to one of your e-mail groups and, within a few minutes, an abundance of information about the subject will start pouring in.

Recently, a subscriber to one of our groups wanted to know about varieties of jasmine bushes and where they grew. Within minutes she had the names of at least four varieties and the times of day or night when they were in bloom.

If you have a subject about which you plan to write and would like quotes from others, you can get them by putting the word out on the Internet. You can do this both through your e-mail groups and on your website.

High Speed Internet Connections

Having a high-speed internet connection (cable or DSL) is all-important. If it is available, see what the cost will be to get it in your location. However, in designing a website, it is essential to remember that many, probably most, visitors to your site will not have high-speed connections. That means you must have a site that is easy to navigate and will download quickly. Most visitors will not wait around to look at slow-loading content. Like you, they just don't have the time. (For more information, see Chapter 13 "Website Magic" by Carl and Jenny Loveland.)

Using the Internet to Advertise

Perhaps you will want a gimmick to draw visitors to your website. Do you have an exciting new recipe to share? Do you have a giveaway or contest for your books? Readers love attractive bookmarks. Perhaps you can offer to mail them one if they send you a stamped, self-addressed envelope.

Your website is your promotional material. It is the advertisement for you and your work. Make it fun, make it exciting, and, most of all, keep it up-to-date. That will inspire visitors to

146

come back.

Also make certain you provide keywords for search engines. Amazon has "A9 Web Search" at the top of its welcome page. Insert your name and not only will you pull up web results, but a column on the right will display thumbnails of images from your sites. Seeing an array of your book covers, photographs, and other artwork is exciting. It can provide an additional avenue of promotion for your work. In addition, A9 has a "site info" button by each web result that includes information about traffic rank, sites that link, speed, and when the site came online. The button also pulls up information about where people who visited that site also have been on the Internet.

The ever-expanding Internet has created a completely new world for writers and artists of all kinds. Enjoy it all.

"I cannot live without books."

Thomas Jefferson, letter to John Adams
June 10, 1815

CHAPTER THIRTEEN

Website Magic

by Carl and Jenny Loveland

The creation of moveable type in the 15th century made a significant difference to authors in their ability to market their ideas. So has the Internet today.

The *magic* that authors must use to market their books is no different now than it was in the 15th century. They must use all available tools to get their ideas to the marketplace.

Website magic is nothing more than e-commerce. The magic is in the just doing it and not leaving it to others.

Authors in the 21st century must be entrepreneurs; that means being a business; that means e-commerce.

Are you ready to "just do it"? If so, continue to read this chapter. If not, skip ahead to the next chapter.

E-commerce Levels

Think of e-commerce like a ladder with four steps or levels. The higher you go on the ladder, the more competitive you are in the 21st century e-commerce business environment. The four levels of e-commerce are:
1. Presence—Simply having an electronic presence, which should feature an e-mail address or, better yet, a website.
2. Interaction—The ability to respond or interact with website visitors or clients, in a manner of their choosing.
3. Promotion—Using electronic tools to promote your ideas (book, etc).
4. Transaction—Completing your transactions electronically. Remember, making sales keeps you in business.

Presence Level

The presence level is nothing more than getting on the e-commerce playing field. The minimum requirement to participate in e-commerce is to have an e-mail address (me@yahoo.com). Do you know anyone today who does not have an e-mail address? If you want to be successful, you really need to go beyond e-mail and develop your own website.

The normal requirement to participate in e-commerce is your own website. A website today means credibility. Most customers think that if you don't have a website you are not a real business—simple as that. A website enhances and extends your brand of work. Here are a couple of examples of author websites:

www.AlinaAdams.com

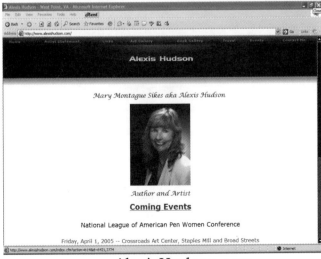

www.AlexisHudson.com

Interaction Level

The interaction level is nothing more than an electronic conversation between buyer and seller—a concept as old as mankind. The only thing different is the medium—the Internet.

Once website visitors or clients are interested in your product or service, they want to begin to have a conversation (interaction) with you. The second step or level on the e-commerce ladder is to be able to interact.

This interaction can be as simple as a "Contact Us" button or as fancy as "Live Support," but the end result is the same—buyers and sellers interacting.

A "Contact Us" feature allows website visitors to contact you anytime, 24/7.

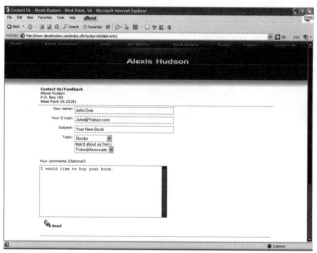

Contact Us form

Promotion Level

Promoting your literary business can be much easier and far less costly using the Internet instead of other methods of advertising. Think of your website promotion features simply as a modern printing press and distribution system.

Think of your website as a business growth tool. Create it. Develop it. Refine it. Refine it again and again and again. Never stop sharpening your business promotion tool—your website.

A calendar feature allows the author to display upcoming events. Don't be shy about including affiliated events (literary associations, art associations, community events, etc). You want website visitors to know you are active and involved in literature and in your community.

Calendar of Events

Each calendar event can provide enhanced detail for the reader. This detail is limited only by your creativity. Examples include:
- Directions or map to the event
- Agenda (may include links to speaker bio, business website, etc)
- Automated RSVP
- Automated reminder
- And much more

The calendar event shown is an example of a writer who is also an artist. This is a regional art event listing that provides information about the event, other artists, and the regional art center. All of these other bits of information may sell not only her art, but also her books.

As you promote your writing business, consider developing relationships with other business owners who can help you promote your business.

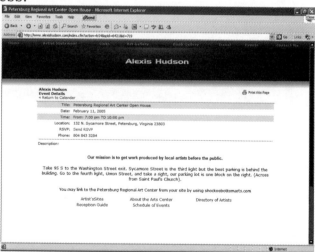

Calendar Event Detail

A Book Gallery offers your website visitor the opportunity to see all your literary products. The beauty of the Internet is that you are not limited by space.

You have the ability to give the visitor as much of a preview of your work as you wish. Today, we see authors electronically providing the Table of Contents and a sample chapter at the click of a mouse.

You may even want to offer your entire book in electronic format and sell it from your website store. (See more about that later in this chapter.)

Additionally, you may want to consider linking to other writers' websites. Do you belong to a writers group? If group members agree, each writer's website can cross-link to other group member websites.

The objective is to help each other grow your business. Just do it!

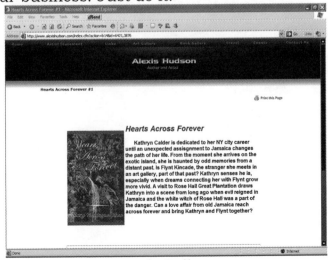

Book Gallery

A newsletter is a powerful tool to market your books and ideas to the world. Yours can be published monthly, quarterly, yearly, or when you publish a book. That's the beauty of electronic newsletters.

If you are interested and work at it, you will be able to gather more e-mail addresses than you can envision.

Imagine if a group of 100 businesses (writers, artists, etc.) each contributed only 100 e-mail addresses into a group newsletter. The result would be a newsletter subscriber list of 10,000 receiving news about your product.

Additionally, newsletter reporting is now so sophisticated that you can "see" whenever each newsletter is opened.

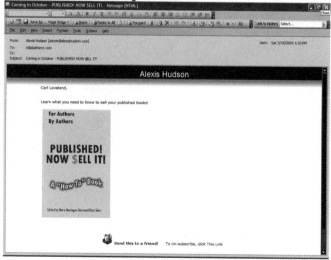

New Book E-newsletter

Transaction Level

A website store can be your entry into a whole new world of transactions. A website store is the 21st century version of a retail storefront.

Authors may now sell their books directly to consumers from their websites. Setting up a website store can be simple.

PayPal is now used by over 63 million small business owners to sell their products and services online:

- For Buyers
  - Choose to pay using your credit card, debit card, or bank account
  - Make secure purchases without revealing your credit card number or financial information
  - Shop using PayPal on eBay and with thousands of merchants worldwide
- For Sellers
  - Accept credit cards, debit cards, and bank account payments for low transaction fees
  - Add PayPal to your website in minutes, no downtime required
  - Get access to a growing user base with millions of active online shoppers

If you want to go even further and get a commercial merchant account, you will need to use a merchant account provider, such a Cardservice International. Cardservice International provides the expertise and reliability to enable merchants to accept credit cards, debit cards, and checks. From the establishment of a merchant account to our technologically sophisticated LinkPoint® Secure Payment Gateway, Cardservice provides a one-stop shop for all types of transaction processing.

Regardless of the type of payment system you choose (PayPal or merchant account) you will be able to complete transactions online. Remember transactions keep you in business.

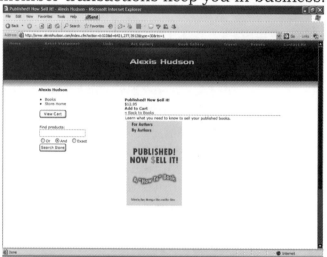
Website Store

Website Considerations

Your website can be a very valuable asset to your business. As you start or develop an existing website, here are a few issues to consider:

- Host—Select a website host that provides these key services:

  1. Choice/Flexibility—Your first website should not be too large or powerful. Select

a website host that allows easy and convenient website upgrade when you are ready, not before.

2. Self Service Administration—Website administration can now be accomplished by us "non-technical" folks. If you operate Microsoft Office software comfortably, you should be able to administer your own website.

- Keywords – Every website owner knows what the keywords are that describe their business. Develop and continue to refine your list of keywords that clients will be searching for when you want them to find your website, product, or service. A good website host will provide the self-service tools to allow you to create and edit your keywords on a regular basis.
- Search Engine Optimization – A feature that can now be accomplished by the administrator.
- Search Engine Submission – Ask your website host how they can help you make sure your website has been submitted or found and indexed by key search engines (Google, Yahoo, etc.)

3. Value—Websites tend to be priced like cell phones. Monthly prices stay just about level, but additional features seem

to get added just about every day. Make sure your website host has an ongoing feature enhancement program.

4. Design—A good website hosting company will have several hundred website design templates that are normally acceptable to the new website owner. The cost is nominal and sometimes free, depending on website purchased.

5. Cost—Variable, but most small business website costs average $15-$75 per month.

- Features

1. Custom URL (Domain)—This is your website "address". Make sure it is a custom/unique domain and not a sub-domain (see below). Additionally, make sure you are the registered domain owner. There have been horror stories of business owners being held "hostage" by domain hosts when the owners thought they owned their domain but, in fact, they did not.

2. Pages—Websites can range from a one-page website to those with an unlimited number of pages. Don't purchase more capability than you need. Remember, when you need additional website features, or pages, you should be able to upgrade easily.

3. Web-based e-mail—In today's mobile world, we are all traveling more and more. Your e-mail should go with you. Web-based e-mail is simply your e-mail that you access from the web.

4. Auto-respond/forward—When you are out of the office you can let e-mail senders know by using auto-respond. It's like a telephone answering machine for your e-mail.

5. Statistics—Real time information can be valuable. Website statistics can provide the number of visitors, pages viewed, length of stay, originating location, type of browser, and many more details.

6. Content Management—Self-service content management can be a powerful, yet easy to use set of tools that should be behind a password protected area. Website control functions as well as content should be easily available to the administrator. No programming expertise should be needed. Website support should include upload of PDF, Word, Excel, Flash, or PowerPoint file types.

7. Calendar—Calendar should display special events for your business. Each calendar event should have up to a full page describing the event. An e-mail RSVP system can be included and any event can be linked to Reservations. Visitors should be able to receive a Reminder E-Mail up to three days prior to an event.

8. Contact Us—A powerful e-mail system that allows you to create numerous topics for clients to select. Multiple e-mail addresses should be available to assign to each topic, if desired.

9. Photo Gallery—Create photo albums with a large number of photos in each

album. Slideshow tools can automatically present photos in a show format.

10. Web Conference—You can conduct presentations via the Internet, display files or internet sites, and share work space. The presentation should be branded to your business.

11. Online Coupons—Offer discount coupons without the high cost of printing and mailing. Coupons can have start and end dates, allowing targeted specials. This feature should include a coupon builder tool to assist the novice.

12. E-forms—This is a very powerful feature that enables you to design custom forms for any business need and have the information sent to any e-mail address. You can download submitted data to CSV or XML format. Some hosts offer Secure E-form Field that allows transfer of secure data over open e-mail.

13. Sub-Domains—URL addresses that link directly to specified content. For example: www.yourdomain.com/clearance on your website.

14. E-newsletters—The E-newsletter potential is limitless. Send HTML formatted newsletters to subscriber lists or individual addressees. Tracking reports may be available showing who opened your message, when, and how many times. A few hosts include a Marketing Campaign tool and can automatically build subscriber lists from E-Form information

15. E-commerce—An online store to offer products and services. Separate departments are normally available to organize merchandise and include a picture. Many now include PayPal® for immediate online payments. Optional Merchant Account may be available. Product Search, Tax/Shipping Computation, Subscription, Digital Delivery, External Products, Inventory, and Transaction Reports are sample features that may be available.

16. Syndication—There are three powerful syndication tools now becoming available to improve your website content by publishing pages with external syndicated feeds, building syndicated web pages from the online catalog of articles, or syndicating your original content out to other users. This is simple, menu driven.

17. Appointments/Reservations—Accept appointments and reservations online at your website. Multiple providers and multiple time periods can be linked to the site calendar. You and your client get a confirmation e-mail when an appointment or reservation is made.

18. Live Support—One click and your customers open a live chat with you or your operator. No software to load. This is initiated from an icon on your website.

19. Intranet/Extranet—If you are a larger business, you can manage staff access to the administrative areas of your website which includes intranet function. This

provides password protected content for clients with add-on extranet capability.

- Emerging Enhancements – These are features you may want to ask your prospective host if they offer.
1. Blogs—Short for *Web Log,* a blog is a Web page that serves as a publicly accessible personal journal for an individual. Typically updated daily, blogs often reflect the personality of the author. A blogger is a person who blogs.

Next Steps

The next steps are simply to "just do it." Don't worry, it is not hard, and authors are doing it more every day.

The basic steps you will need to accomplish are:

1. Establish your own vision for the website project—this is the hard part.
   a. Talk to other authors
   b. Talk to business solutions providers (see below)
   c. Visit author websites. This can be a great help in defining your vision.
2. Identify a business solutions provider—anyone can offer you a website, but a business solutions provider will be able to offer an online system of integrated tools to help you make your website project a long term success.
3. Get moving!

Resources

Business Growth
> *Dash One*
> P.O. Box 8131
> Yorktown, VA 23693
> Tel: 757-989-0714
> www.DashOne.com

Design
> *Allwebco Design*
> www.Allwebcodesign.com

Transactions
> PayPal
> www.PayPal.com
> Cardservice International
> www.Cardservicesales.com

Technology Terms
> Webopedia
> www.webopedia.com

Book Marketing
> Free Book Marketing
> https://print.google.com/publisher/?hl=en_US
> Book Marketing and Promotion
> http://www.bookmarket.com
> Book Marketing Tip of the Week
> http://www.bookmarket.com/tips.html

About Us

Jenny & Carl Loveland

We are probably just like you. We are "boomers" who have lived full and active lives. Here is a bit more about us:

- Our Backgrounds
  - Jenny was born in Japan and was raised in California. She has three college degrees, including one from UC Berkeley in the 1970s. She completed her first career as an Air Force officer.
  - Carl was born in Washington and raised in California. He has two college degrees, one in finance and one in public administration. He completed his first career as an Air Force officer.
- Our Current Projects
  - Art – Jenny is the artist in our family. She enjoys painting, but she is learning that art is a business. She has developed and continued to refine her Moonlit Art Studio website. She recently sent out an e-newsletter announcing her recent works and sold a painting within hours.
  - Technology – Carl is the organizer in our family. His passion is the understanding of how internet technology can be organized for the benefit of an individual community

and the businesses within that community. Historically, individual community economies were insulated by distance. Today, that has changed. Community Networks are being created and developed around the world to help local economic and community development.

- o Community Service – We both feel community service is important. We serve today through participation on boards of directors and as website administrators.
- Our Websites
  - o LovelandGroup.com
  - o MoonlitArtStudio.com
  - o DashOne.com
  - o PreferredProviderNetworks.com
  - o SkyCross.com
- Our Family
  - o 5 great kids!
- Our e-mail addresses
  - o Jenny@LovelandGroup.com
    CL@LovelandGroup.com

"The mass of men lead lives of quiet desperation."

Henry David Thoreau, *Walden*

CHAPTER FOURTEEN

Getting Book Reviews

by Mary Montague Sikes

How important are book reviews for your sales success? Immensely.

Getting good reviews in the right places can mean thousands of dollars worth of book sales. One of the most important review locations for a writer is *Publisher's Weekly* magazine.

My publisher announced the publication of *Hotels to Remember* in *Publisher's Weekly*. However, a galley or review copy was never sent to *Publisher's Weekly*, hence my book received no review by them. Even had we sent a review copy, a review of my book would not necessarily have been written. Unfortunately for the writer, only about 20 percent, or fewer, of the books that this periodical receives are actually reviewed.

Although reviewers for the *New York Times Book Review* section may review only one in ten books submitted to them, it is still a good idea for you to send them a copy of your book along with a personal letter that points out something unique about you or your work. A good review from the *Times* will add importance to your website, media kit, and to you as a professional. A well-written personal letter sent along with the book might just help you get that review.

Other major newspaper book review sections may have an interest in your book, especially if you can establish a connection with the cities involved. Some possibilities are: *The Washington Post, Chicago Tribune, Miami Herald, Los Angeles Times, St. Louis Post-Dispatch,* etc. And don't forget to submit your book along with a personal letter to *USA Today*.

Midwest Book Review (Jim Cox) gave *Hotels to Remember* a nice review that is displayed on the Amazon website. Cox is a well-recognized reviewer, so if you can score a good review from him it is well worth the effort. To submit, you will need to send a published copy of your book.

Submit a Review Copy Six Months Prior to Publication

The importance of submitting a review copy three to six months prior to publication cannot be overemphasized. That is especially true if you wish to connect with the library market.

Reviews in *Library Journal* are an important tool for librarians to use in deciding which books to purchase. A superior review there may result in many additional sales to libraries. According to its website http://www.libraryjournal.com, *Library Journal* offers professional reviews of 6000 titles from the approximately 40,000 books received each year. Manuscripts, galleys, and page proofs sent three to four months prior to publication are acceptable as submissions. Small publishers may send a finished book as long as it arrives several months before the publication of the book. *Booklist* receives more than 60,000 submissions a year. From that number, the magazine reviews 4000 adult books, 2500 children's books, and 500 reference books. Submit galleys 15 weeks prior to the publication date.

If you wish to give rank to the importance of reviews on a site, you may want to look on www.amazon.com. *Publisher's Weekly, Library Journal,* and *Booklist* appear in that order for a book by one of my favorite authors, Deborah Smith.

Search for Review Sites on the Internet

There are many sites on the Internet where you may place requests for book reviews. ReviewersChoice-subscribe@yahoogroups.com is one. Authors write summaries of their books and give other basic information when they request reviews. Another place for book reviews is www.NewAndUsedBooks.com. This is a well-maintained site that regularly sends out newsletters describing new releases to subscribers.

You can find more internet book reviewers by putting "book reviews" into a search engine like Google or Dogpile. That's how I found BookPage, which has a monthly online edition. One recent issue included 61 book reviews, focusing on books about cooking, suspense, and romance.

Look at reviews on www.amazon.com. Read some of the book reviews there and pick out reviewers you particularly like. Choose one of them, then select "see all my reviews" for that reviewer. After reading through his/her reviews, you may decide you would like to have your book reviewed by that person if possible.

See who the best reviewers are for Amazon. They rank their reviewers and have them listed on the site.

Recently, Harriet Klausner, a former acquisitions librarian, had the number one ranking for Amazon reviewers. At that time, Klausner, a speed-reader who reads two books a day, had reviewed 8370 books for Amazon. You may want to ask Klausner or someone else on the list, which numbers in the thousands of reviewers, to review your book.

No matter where you go on the Internet, you seem to eventually get directed to the Amazon website since many book services are tied into that company's site. The Borders site is connected to Amazon.

There are countless reviewers on the Internet. You need to take the time to look and to study where you can get the best and most professional reviews for your work.

Newspaper Reviews

Don't forget your own local newspapers. Not only may they review your book, but they may also do a feature story on you as a local personality.

Not long ago, a writer I know from an internet group published her first novel and was interviewed about it by her local newspaper. The editor liked her work so much that he asked if she would be interested in writing a weekly personal experience column. She accepted, has since written many columns for that newspaper, and has become well-known in her state.

Follow-up, Shipping, and More

Many reviewers are available for your books. You may contact them by e-mail or regular mail. If you don't hear back from them within a reasonable time, then make a follow-up telephone call.

When you are ready to ship your book, pack it with care and ship using the media mailing rate with the United States Postal Service. You can print out your own delivery confirmation label from your computer for free. Then check the tracking number to make certain it arrives safely.

Whether or not a review is favorable, always remember to write a personal note to your reviewer. It is often said that any publicity is good publicity.

As with everything in the publishing business, take time, do research, and sell yourself and your book to your reviewers.

Take advantage of all opportunities. You have little to lose and a lot to gain in book sales and name recognition.

CHAPTER FIFTEEN

The Business of Writing

by Jean C. Keating
and Mildred H. B. Roberson

Writing is an art and a craft, but it is also a business. Irrespective of the method by which a writer is published, income from sales of that writing must be reported for taxes. If you are reading this book, you are not a writer who ignores sales. You accept that the business of finding readers who will buy your book is your concern. The business of recordkeeping and reporting of sales, income and sales taxes due, deductible expenses, and hopefully net gains is all your concern. The information you collect, document, and validate must support income, sales and inventory tax reported.

The following topics reflect our experiences

with the business part of writing. We hope what we have learned along the way may help you as you develop your own business of writing.

Income Taxes

Early in the game you need to get the Federal Internal Revenue Service pamphlets pertaining to conducting a business. Since tax laws can change frequently, you'll need to get updated pamphlets each year. Some writers feel comfortable in doing their own taxes and use off-the-shelf software to prepare their tax returns. Others find that the $250-$300 yearly fee for a good tax accountant is well worth the money. Whichever way you decide is right for you, you need to keep accurate records of expenses and receipts documented with date, method of payment, and reason for the deduction as well as a careful list of income received.

Sales Taxes

If your state or township has a sales tax, you will need even more records relating to such taxes. This will vary according to the way in which you are published and will be discussed in more detail below.

Recordkeeping and Reporting

The amount of recordkeeping necessary for each author will vary according to the way in which each author is published. The three examples that follow show some of the differences in business records involved for authors who publish with large publishing houses, with a print-on-demand publisher, and who are self-published.

Recordkeeping when Published by Major or Small Publishing Houses

Writers will have signed a contract that gives the publisher most or all of the rights to their work in return for an advance and a promise of royalties on books sold that exceed the advance. The publisher handles sales to bookstores and on-line book dealers like Amazon.com. Usually, the writer's account is charged back for any listings made in magazines announcing new books in print. A business license is usually not required; neither are arrangements to pay sales tax.

Promotion by the writer is usually limited to arrangements for book signings at retail locations. Sales personnel there collect state tax on books that they order directly from the publisher. Expenses that are not paid by the publishing house for these signings are an income tax deduction. Publishing houses pay few expenses for beginning and mid-list writers. Many writers utilize most of their first advance to market their books, in phone calls to make arrangements for appearances to promote their books, in travel promoting their books, in creating bookmarks and other promotional materials, and in ads in magazines appropriate for their genres to publicize their books.

Recordkeeping when Published with a Print-on-demand Company

Business records must be more extensive when a writer utilizes a print-on-demand company to produce their work. Any book accepted for sale by booksellers (conventional stores or on-line electronic ones) must contain an ISBN, the first eight digits of which indicate the publisher, and the last two of which indicate the specific book and printing. Most print-on-demand companies furnish this number for the writer. A writer who chooses to publish through a print-on-demand company is spared the necessity of applying to Bowker and getting an ISBN for their book. Print-on-demand companies also handle the sales to bookstores, arrange for the listing of the book on Amazon.com and handle the sales to these bookstores and on-line booksellers. Print-on-demand companies will vary in what they do, so writers should review carefully the services being offered. Most provide quarterly lists of books sold, prices at which these were sold, and a quarterly check for writer's earnings.

The writer is a good deal more involved in sales and promotion to individuals and to independent bookstores than are those who publish through a major publishing company. But then they retain all rights to their book.

Writers who utilize print-on-demand publishing should carefully review the sales tax laws for their states. In Virginia, this situation requires a filing with the Virginia Department of

Taxation for authorization to collect sale taxes. And, of course, this means filing sales tax reports. For the first year or until the Department of Taxation tells you otherwise, a writer is required to file monthly reports on sale taxes collected and owed to the state. And you must file the report, whether or not you sold a single book or owe a penny of tax, or be fined for failure to report. After the first year, the Department of Taxation generally will notify you that only quarterly reports are necessary.

Writers who utilize this method must spend more time on promoting through ads and personal appearances, all of which are deductible if properly documented. Writers may wish to get a business license from the local city or county in which they live. It is not absolutely necessary, but it gives you a business number under which to apply for a permit from your state to collect sales taxes. You can do this, if you choose, under your name and social security number.

If your state charges sales tax, you will need to obtain a permit to charge the tax, record the taxes collected, and pay the taxes to the state. In Virginia, sales to individuals must include sales taxes, but mail orders out of state do not require the collection of a sales tax. Be careful, however, if you do promotional appearances out-of-state in other than established businesses in those states. Book signings in bookstores and businesses in other states count as sales to a third party. You sell to the stores and they sell to the individuals. Sales tax is not an issue since the third party (the established business or bookseller in that state) will be collecting the taxes. If you appear at a fair or special event in another state that has sales tax where you are collecting the money from direct sales to individuals, and you have not arranged to be a temporary collector of sales tax in that state, that state has the right to seize all your wares! So always pay attention to sales tax laws in your own state and in states in which you appear to promote your book.

A writer who has published through print-on-demand must consider carefully the profit margin available on the books before deciding on the most productive means of promotion. The industry standard deduction expected by booksellers is 40 percent. If the margin of profit available to you doesn't leave you with sufficient funds to pay for travel and promotion to booksellers, then you may wish to confine your promotional efforts to direct sales to individuals.

Consider the following example with a print-on-demand company used by one of the authors of this book. The author's book has a list price of $14, but by the terms of publication, she must pay $8 per book in lots of 100 for the book. If she can only get $8.40 (60 percent of list price] in payment from booksellers, then the margin-of-profit of 40¢ per book does not leave enough to cover expenses of travel to book signings. She is better off utilizing her funds to promote direct sales to individuals in which she can recover the full list price on each book.

Recordkeeping for Self-published Books

Writers who self-publish must handle income, sales tax, and inventory records and reporting as well as all promotional efforts. In Virginia, a business license is necessary in the name you've chosen for your publishing company. Other states may vary. Income tax and sales tax reporting issues noted in the segments above apply equally here.

If you are self-published, you will already have a name and an ISBN for your publishing company. Perhaps you will also have a logo for your business. Hopefully, you will have developed your own billing/shipping order form with the name. With today's excellent color printers and computer graphic packages and word processors, shipping orders on each book should be accompanied by a shipping/billing order that shows the name, price, brief description, and ISBN for all of your books. Take advantage of each order you fill to advertise your other books just by the presence of their listing on the shipping order. See the example of a shipping/billing order for Astra Publishers at the end of this chapter. Note the brief description of each book available that is transmitted with an order for any one of them. Develop your own logo and use the name prominently on each order. It is one more way to get the name and logo of your business known.

A cash method of accounting is recommended. Keep two separate, though related, tabulations for orders placed and cash received. The file of orders and the amount charged for each order are necessary to reflect inventory movement and to keep track of outstanding bills as well as those paid. However, while individual orders may be paid up front and some booksellers and internet buyers will pay immediately, slow payers may require money received to be placed into different quarters for income and sales tax reporting. This is the first reason for separating the orders from the payments.

The second is the way Amazon.com pays. Amazon.com pays on the number of your books they sell each month, sending a bank deposit to your account. Their payments do not reflect their orders or your shipments during a month or quarter, only the sales of your books by Amazon during the month.

You must report a check received as income when you receive it, not when you finally send it to your bank. But in a cash method, of accounting you need not report payments/income until they are received. The cash method of accounting is especially helpful when book orderers keep books for some time and then return them without payment. In such cases, by using the cash accounting method you need to adjust your inventory but need not make adjustments to your income reporting, since you received no payment.

Conclusions

Whatever the method of publishing by which your work has been produced, keep good records of income, sales, and expenditures with dates, explanations, and supportive paperwork. Stay abreast of yearly changes in tax laws and if necessary consult an experienced tax accountant.

Published! Now Sell It!

Astra Publishers

209 Matoaka Court, Williamsburg, VA 23185 [757] 220-3385, info@astrapublishers.com, www.astrapublishers.com

Billing/Shipping Invoice

Date of Invoice: December 12, 2004   **Invoice Number:** AP04.093

* *

Purchased by: Amazon.Com Advantage DC   **Bill to:** not required
                    1850 Mercer Drive
                    Lexington, KY 40511

Customer's Purchase Order Number: L9405989   **Date Received:** Dec. 11, 2004

* *

Shipment Information:
    Date shipped: December 13, 2004
    Method of shipment: Media mail
    Terms of payment: paid by publisher

* *

Description of Order	Price	Quantity	Cost
Amorous Accident: A Dog's Eye View of Murder by Jean C. Keating ISBN 0-9674016-0-7 Paperback, 284 pages Mystery featuring Papillon named Sky	$12.99	0	00.00
Pawprints On My Heart by Jean C. Keating and Beverly S. Abbott ISBN 0-9674016-1-5 Hardback, 189 pages illustrated Short stories about animals, 57 b/w illustrations	$19.99	3	59.97
Paw Prints Through The Years by Jean C. Keating and Beverly S. Abbott ISBN 0-9774016-3-1 Hardback, 224 pages Life with six generations of Papillons, 8 color pages of Papillons	$28.00	0	00.00

Subtotal of order ....   XX.XX
Sales Tax if applicable: ....   N/A
Discount: xx% ....   XX.XX
Shipping and handling charges: ....   N/A
Total order: Paid ___ Owed _X___ ....   XX.XX

* *

Please include invoice number on check and remit amount owed to:
                    Astra Publishers
                    209 Matoaka Court
                    Williamsburg, VA 23185

CHAPTER SIXTEEN

Putting Together the Total Package: A Plan of Promotion

by Mary Montague Sikes

Your beautiful book has been published, and now you are holding it in your hands. Your name is on the cover, and you can hardly wait to see that name gleaming from the shelf of your favorite bookstore.

Easy?

No. Not easy at all.

That is, unless you are a big name celebrity or your large publishing house has chosen you for a special promotional thrust. The latter could happen, but it is highly unlikely.

If you are mid-list with a big publisher, you will be on your own. If you are with a small publishing house, you are on your own as well. Of course, if you are self-published, you already know it's all up to you.

That's why you need a marketing plan.

You Need a Marketing Plan

With the contract of my first book, *Hearts Across Forever* came a marketing plan questionnaire from my publisher. I was surprised. Why did I need a marketing plan?

One of the first questions on the questionnaire was, "Who will read this book?"

Since my book is a reincarnation-related story set in Jamaica and is connected to the legend of the "White Witch of Rose Hall," I thought I knew my audience pretty well.

People who had vacationed in Jamaica would want to read it—especially if they had visited the intriguing Rose Hall Great House around which much of the story is centered. People in Jamaica familiar with the White Witch of Rose Hall Legend would be interested. So would those who travel on cruise ships in the Caribbean. And people who toy with the idea of reincarnation and are curious about it would enjoy my book.

But how would I let them know it even existed? That was the next question on my publisher's form.

I had lots of ideas. Of course, I would contact Rose Hall. Then I would contact major Jamaican hotels, the Jamaican tourist bureau, and Air Jamaica. I would do all these things while I completed the coffee table book on which I was working. Of course, I also would have time left over for the three part-time jobs I held and for my career as an artist as well.

Unfortunately, there was not enough time left in the day or in the week to accomplish all of this. Something had to go, and it was my marketing job for *Hearts Across Forever.*

The truth of the matter was I had not made a real, organized marketing plan. I needed to go back to square one and plan my marketing time.

A writer friend told me she spent two days on marketing for every day she wrote. To be successful, that's what it takes, she said.

I knew she was right, but I also knew I did not have that much time. For my own schedule, my part-time jobs usually require three days a week of my time.

By now, I had two books to promote, one fiction, one nonfiction. Both needed to be sent out for book reviews. I found that while newspapers in the cities where hotels from *Hotels to Remember* are located were willing to review my book, the same papers were not interested in my novel.

Because *Hotels to Remember* has a segment in Jamaica, my two books could be connected for promotion in that location. But would it be practical to promote it there?

With limited time and resources for promotion, practicality can become a major issue. That is why creating a plan of promotion well ahead of time is essential.

A Plan of Promotion

Begin promotion as soon as your book is accepted for publication.

If you are self-publishing, you need to consider also the difference between print date and publication date. The print date is the day the book is actually printed. The publication date is an arbitrary date after the print date (usually six months later) by which time all the "buzz" and publicity should have made the book a success.

Six Months Prior to Publication

The following are things you should begin to plan and do *six months or more prior to publication.* Allocate at least two hours a day for these promotional activities.

1. Put out a press release. This should be about you and your book. Send it to newspapers, e-mail lists, e-newsletters—any place where you have a connection or the subject of your book might have a connection. You may want also to send your press release to an online free distribution service such as www.PRWeb.com. That site has helpful information about how to write a press release and what should be included in it. The site will also connect you to www.prwebdirect.com, which offers more services and faster expanded press release distribution for a fee. Another free press release distribution site is www.pressbox.co.uk

2. Join professional organizations. This will help you gain recognition as a serious professional in the field of writing. For my romance novel, I was already a member of Romance Writers of America (RWA) as well as three affiliate chapters of that group. In addition, I belong to four different writers' groups in Virginia. Most of these groups have e-mail lists that provide a great deal of support information and opportunities to communicate with other authors for answers to questions.

In hindsight, I should have joined some travel writers' organizations prior to publication of my book, *Hotels to Remember*. Authors with a niche book such as that one should consider affiliation with clubs in their specialty fields.

3. Add a line in your e-mail signature. When you communicate with members of your writers groups, be sure to place the name of your book, name of publisher, and the release date beneath your signature. For example:

Mary Good Writer
www.marygoodwriter.com
My Life Story, Good Writer Press

4. Purchase a Day Planner. Find a nice looking leather bound day planner with extra plastic sleeves inside it. You can carry your business cards, bookmarks, book cover copies, press releases, photographs taken at book signings, and much more inside this valuable little case. Carry it with you everywhere you go,

and distribute your cards and other information to the people you meet. Ask about leaving some of your bookmarks on the counter at your favorite bookstore. Readers love to collect them and that will lead to more sales.

5. Join the local Chamber of Commerce (or its equivalent). Attend meetings. Get to know the people, and always take your day planner along with you. Let your new friends know about the progress of your book.

6. Create new business cards. You can make them yourself on your computer using photo quality card blanks put out by Avery. Be sure to include the title and release date of your new book. Include either a photo of yourself or of your book cover on the card.

Also, design a letterhead that promotes you and your book. You might want to create an array of posters and other items that relate to your letterhead logo and can be used for displays at book signings, talks, and other events where you and your work are featured.

7. Get endorsements for your book. Do you have an author friend who will read your manuscript and write a brief endorsement for it? Better yet, do you have a connection through one of your writers groups with someone well known in a field related to your book? If so, approach them now and get those endorsements for the front or back covers of your book.

8. Build up a website. If you do not have one already, create a clean, good-looking website with your new book the center of attention. Write a brief description of the book. If you have endorsements, include a link to a page featuring them. You may want a website for your book as well. My publisher set up a website for *Hotels to Remember.* If you have a website for your book, you need to let people know by using it on business cards, press releases, and in all correspondence you send out. You also will need to allow time to update any websites you have.

9. Make up review copies (galleys) of your book and get them out three to six months prior to publication. You need to include the words "uncorrected proof" on the copy as well as the ISBN, publisher's contact information, publication date, a brief description of the book and its author(s), and more. If you have a publicist, list the contact information.

Publisher's Weekly, Kirkus Reviews (2 copies), *Foreword Magazine,* and *Midwest Book Reviews* are among the most important review contacts. Also, be sure to send review copies to any newspaper that may relate to the book subject (especially if it is travel) or to which the author has a connection.

Contact on-line reviewers and send copies to them for review. Include New and Used Books http://www.newandusedbooks.com. Also include ReviewersChoice@yahoogroups.com. You can find many more on-line reviewers by checking the Internet.

Send a published copy of your book to reviewers at professional organizations to which you belong. *Hotels to Remember* was reviewed by the College of William and Mary's alumni magazine, but Mary Washington College, from which I hold an undergraduate degree, did not review my book. This illustrates how difficult it may be to get your work reviewed and shows the importance of starting early.

10. Write a magazine article about a topic from your book. Some local or regional magazines will welcome a story as a tradeoff for unused advertising space. You may get an ad for your book to go along with your articles. Since you are an expert on your subject, you can get paid for articles written about it.

Three Months Prior to Publication

At least three months prior to publication, do the following.

1. List with wholesale distributors. These will include Ingram, Baker and Taylor, New Leaf for New Age books, and Quality Books, Inc., which has a sales group that markets to libraries.

2. Start booking radio and television appearances. You have created buzz about your book, now start showing off yourself and your product through popular media programs. It may take some time to get on a schedule, so start now. Your book may already be in print by

the time you appear, so you will have it in hand to discuss.

3. Begin to approach libraries, community colleges, bookstores, and chain stores in your area about book signings and speaking engagements. Make a list of topics you are qualified to discuss and offer to speak on a subject of their choice. Besides getting to publicize your book, you may be paid a speaker's fee—a nice way to supplement your writing income.

4. Create an e-mail newsletter and have it ready to send out right before the release of your book. Include a brief synopsis of your new book. Also, be sure to note your endorsements. This is a good time to create a contest and offer an autographed copy of your new book as the prize.

Keep the Buzz Going

Throughout all the exciting days and weeks prior to publication of your new book, create your own buzz about it and keep it going. Do this with your newspaper press releases, visits to bookstores, contacts with your friends and associates, and much more.

Make a list of everything you need to do to promote your special book. Create a day-by-day timeline for that promotion, and work to keep within that timeline.

Above all, don't forget to begin writing your next book. If your new writing project has a connection to the book you are promoting, use that fact as a hook for readers who will want to see more of your work.

Long before you have it ready for market, your new readers will start asking about the release date for your next book, so be prepared. Be ready to continue the buzz!

Appendix

Author Biographies

There are a total of five authors who have contributed to the realization of *Published! Now Sell It!* Their biographies appear on the following pages.

Joseph Guion

E.R. Kallus

Jean C. Keating

Mildred H. B. Roberson

Mary Montague Sikes

Joseph Guion

Joseph E. Guion enlisted in the U.S. Navy in 1943 and retired as a commander in 1973. He served as the commanding officer of four Navy ships and an overseas shore command. He holds a BA in economics from Kings College, and a master's degree in management from the U.S. Navy Postgraduate School. He taught at Tidewater Community College for nine years and resigned as an associate professor of business to concentrate on serving the Catholic Church. He also served as an adjunct lecturer for Golden Gate University.

His book, *Love Songs on the Journey,* ISBN 0-9724165-0-1, consists of poems and reflections on love during one's life journey to and with God. The core of it stems from 50 years of married love with his late wife, Madge, and their family. The market is for people who love, have loved, or will love.

His extensive experience in church leadership positions at the diocesan and parish level has broadened his understanding of life's journey. Guion has facilitated spiritual retreats and workshops for parish leadership groups since 1982, with emphasis on the need to love one another as a focus for service. He is currently chairperson of the Diocesan Pastoral Council, one of the two main consultative groups serving the bishop in the Diocese of Richmond. In 2002, he received the Papal Benemerenti medal for service to the Catholic Church.

Mr. and Mrs. Guion started a Children's Liturgy of the Word program at Saint Gregory's parish in Virginia Beach. Guion designed a program that provides lesson plans for teachers, original songs, weekly handouts with home activity, original puppet scripts to enhance interest, and a banner that proclaims the week's gospel in text and pictures. The final banner panels depict children acting out the Gospel message. Several parishes have used this program with great success.

Guion is seeking an agent or publisher for a recently completed novel, *The Savior.*

Guion is an active member at Saint Bede's Catholic Church in Williamsburg. He serves on the board of the Chesapeake Bay Writers Club and is a member of the Virginia Poets Society and the Emerson Society in Williamsburg.

E. R. Kallus

E. R. Kallus writes primarily about flying, aviation history, military history, and travel. His first novel is *Denial of* Solace, an expose of navy medicine. His second book *Danny in the Liar's Den,* a historical novel that is the story of a young horse cavalry officer in the Rio Grande Valley, is nearing completion. He's a collaborating author of *Published! Now Sell It!*

His love affair with words was sparked under the stern tutelage of Rosa Meinecke, *the* classic old maid English teacher. It was further ignited by an avid interest in history and the experiences of two careers: one as a naval aviator who, during an exile in the Pentagon, discovered a love of writing; the second as an airline pilot.

He's a member of the Chesapeake Writers Club and the California Writers Club. For several years he was a staffer for the *California Historical Society Quarterly.*

If there's anything Kallus likes better than writing, it's traveling. Most of it has been to Europe, but he's visited every continent except Antarctica. His happiest days away from home are those when he can mingle with the locals and persuade them, however briefly, into thinking he's one of them. He's been successful in the Czech Republic, Germany, Austria, and Spain, but the canny folk in the British Isles spotted him instantly.

Appendix

Kallus is at home amid the natural beauty and historical richness of Virginia's remote Northern Neck, between the Rappahannock and Potomac rivers. He has degrees in Electrical Engineering and History.

Jean C. Keating

Jean C. Keating has been writing novels starring companion animals for five years. In 2004 she was nominated for a Pulitzer Prize for *Paw Prints Through the Years.* This third and latest book by Keating has also been nominated for numerous other national and state awards including the Library of Virginia Literary Award, a National Book Award, and Dog Writers' Association of America's Maxwell Award for Best Dog Fiction.

Keating's second book, *Pawprints on My Heart,* was one of three finalists for Best Dog Fiction of 2001.

Keating holds degrees in mathematics, physics, and information systems. Named Virginia's Outstanding Young Woman of the Year in 1970 for her civic as well as professional efforts as an aerospace engineer with NASA, she authored more than 50 scientific and educational administrative reports during her years with NASA and subsequent service as head of research for Virginia's Higher Education Council.

She retired from government service in 1998, began writing fiction, and formed her own publishing company, Astra Publishers. Her first two books include a mystery set in Williamsburg and Richmond and a collection of short stories about animal companions. Her latest novel chronicles the loves and laughs of living with six generations of her dogs. The voice of the author alternates with whimsical holiday letters from the dogs in which they present their own versions of the human-animal bond.

Keating's short stories have been published in *Pap Pourri, The Write Dog, RT Booknotes* and four editions of *Critique's Choice.* She is a regular contributor to <u>Animal Antics</u> for *Chesapeake Style Magazine.* The immediate past president of the Chesapeake Writers Group, Jean lives in Williamsburg, Virginia, with two cats, an ever changing number of show papillons and rescued dogs, and is busy with her fifth book, the sequel to her mystery entitled *Beguiling Bundle: Death Takes Best of Breed.*

Mildred H. B. Roberson

Mildred H. B. Roberson is a retired professor of nursing with over 40 years combined nursing education, service, and administrative experience. She is also a researcher/scholar of Southern African American health culture with 25 professional publications and has presented numerous papers and speeches at national and international meetings. In 1997, she received the Leininger Transcultural Nursing Award for leadership in the transcultural nursing field.

She obtained her nursing diploma in Boston, her BSN at Case Western Reserve, her MSN in Community Health Nursing at Medical College of Virginia, and her PhD in nursing at the University of Utah. It was while conducting her doctoral research that she met Claudine Curry Smith, a retired midwife, and together they began plans to some day record Mrs. Smith's experiences.

My Bag Was Always Packed: The Life and Times of a Virginia Midwife is the result of their plans. It documents Mrs. Smith's life experiences, as well as the times in which she has lived and practiced.

Dr. Roberson serves on a local museum committee on African American history, a regional board to address area health needs, and a statewide task force on Arthritis. She also tutors in reading locally at the public schools.

She is very active in politics, currently serving as a Precinct Captain.

She, her husband, and their cat live in their home on the bay in Lancaster County VA. The Robersons love being on the water but also enjoy travel. Col. Roberson is a retired fighter pilot who became an ace during World War II and went on to serve 31 years in the Air Force. As a result of his interests, the Robersons go to several aviation meetings around the country every year where they renew old friendships.

Mary Montague Sikes

Mary Montague Sikes is a writer, artist, photographer, and speaker. She has presented writing and art workshops and served as a panel speaker for various groups, including the Virginia Festival of the Book and Christopher Newport University's Writers Conference.

Her award-winning feature articles and photographs have appeared in newspapers and magazines including: the *Miami Herald, Buffalo News, Newport News Daily Press, Southern Boating, BWIA Caribbean Beat, Venture Inward,* and *ASU Travel Guide.*

Sikes' first novel, *Hearts Across Forever,* was a PRISM award finalist and won first place in the National Federation of Press Women 2002 Communications Contest. Reviewer Anne Edwards wrote, "Mary Montague Sikes uses her considerable talent to create a world of mystery and romance. . . . A terrific read that will keep you turning pages."

Her nonfiction book, *Hotels to Remember,* was first place winner in the Virginia Press Women 2003 Communications Contest. "Part-memoir, part-travelogue, *Hotels to Remember* charms the reader at repeated sittings," wrote Barbara Bell Matuszewski, Book Reviews Editor for the *Pen Woman.*

Sikes designed the covers for both *Hotels to Remember* and *Hearts Across Forever* and has designed covers for other books as well. A lover of art, she enjoys designing flyers and brochures to promote her writing and artwork.

Holder of a Master of Fine Arts degree from Virginia Commonwealth University, she studied with New York artists Peter Saul, Jane Kaufman, and Diana Kurz, and California artists Robert Burridge, Elaine Harvey, and Raleigh Kinney.

Intrigued by the Arizona desert and the Indian secrets from ancient times locked in its sands, Sikes has created her next novel, *Eagle Rising*, and set it in one of her favorite locations. Another novel, *Seas of Danger*, situated on the Caribbean island of Antigua, is nearing completion.

When she isn't writing or painting, Sikes enjoys traveling to faraway places, playing tennis, and participating in step aerobics classes. An avid baseball fan, she likes watching her favorite team, the St. Louis Cardinals.

Sikes lives in Virginia where she and her husband Olen are surrounded by woods with a view of scenic marshland and a creek.

Books by Authors of
PUBLISHED! NOW SELL IT!

Guion, Joseph, *Love Songs on the Journey*,
      ISBN 0-9724165-0-1

Keating, Jean C., *Amorous Accident,*
      ISBN 0-9674016-0-7

Keating, Jean C., *Paw Prints on My Heart,*
      ISBN 0-9674016-1-5

Keating, Jean C., *Paw Prints Through the Years,*
      ISBN 0-9674016-3-1

Roberson, Mildred H. B. and Smith, Claudine Curry, *My Bag Was Always Packed: The Life and Times of a Virginia Midwife.*
      ISBN 1-4033-7532-1 (paperback)
      ISBN 1-4033-7531-3 (e-book)

Sikes, Mary Montague, *Hearts Across Forever,*
      ISBN 1-892343-20-7

Sikes, Mary Montague, *Hotels to Remember,*
      ISBN 1-892343-18-5

Author Websites

All authors of *Published! Now Sell It!*
www.bookwaves.net
www.marketplacepublicity.com

Joseph Guion
www.alltap.net

Jean C. Keating
www.Astrapublishers.com

Mary Montague Sikes
www.alexishudson.com
www.marymontaguesikes.com

Resources

Publishers Weekly
360 Park Avenue South
New York, NY 10010
Tel: 646-746-6758
Fax: 646-746-6631
www.publishersweekly.com

Library Journal
360 Park Avenue South
New York, NY 10010
Tel: 646-746-6819
Fax: 646-746-6734
www.libraryjournal.com

Kirkus Reviews
VNU US Literary Group
770 Broadway
New York, NY 10003
www.kirkusreviews.com

Midwest Book Review
James A. Cox
Editor-in-Chief
278 Orchard Drive
Oregon, WI 53575-1129
Tel: 1-608-835-7937
mbr@execpc.com
mwbookrevw@aol.com

National League of American Pen Women
National Headquarters
Pen Arts Building
1300 Seventeenth St., N.W.
Washington, DC 20036-1973
Tel: 202-785-1997
info@americanpenwomen.org

Romance Writers of America, Inc.
16000 Stuebner Airline Rd Suite 140
Spring, TX 77379
Tel: 832.717.5200
Fax: 832.717.5201
info@rwanational.org

National Federation of Press Women
P.O. Box 5556
Arlington, VA 22205
Tel: 800-780-2715
Fax: 703-534-5751
presswomen@aol.com

Southern Scribe
Joyce Dixon
www.southernscribe.com
joyce@southernscribe.com

New and Previously Owned Books
119 Park Avenue
Yakima WA 98902
Tel: 800-930-6762
Tel: 509-453-6762
vickie@newandusedbooks.com

New Leaf Distributing Co.
401 Thornton Rd.
Lithia Springs, GA 30122-1557
Tel: 770-948-7845
Fax: 770-944-2313
www.newleaf-dist.com
newleaf@newleaf-dist.com

Books

Self-Publishing Manual: How to Write, Print and Sell Your Own Book
Dan Poynter
www.ParaPublishing.com

Guerrilla Marketing for Writers
Jay Conrad Levinson, Rick Frishman & Michael Larsen

The Publishing Game: Bestseller in 30 Days
Fern Reiss

Art Marketing 101
Constance Smith

Hot Marketing
Robert and Kate Burridge

How to Give a Damn Good Speech: Even When You Have No Time to Prepare
Philip R. Theibert

*Complete Guide to Self Publishing: Everything
You Need to Know to Write, Publish, Promote, and
Sell Your Own Book*
Tom Ross, Marilyn Ross

*Guerrilla Publicity: Hundreds of Sure-Fire Tactics
to Get Maximum Sales for Minimum Dollars*
Jay Conrad Levinson, Rick Frishman, Jill Lublin

*How to Get on Radio Talk Shows All Across
America Without Leaving Your Home or Office: A
New Way to Promote Yourself, Your Books, Your
Tapes*
Joe Sabah (Only available directly from Joe
Sabah at Pacesetter Publications)
PO Box 101330
Denver, CO 80250
Tel: 303-722-7200 or 1-800-945-2488
Fax: 303-733-2626
JSabah@aol.com
www.sabahradioshows.com/halfprice.htm

Index

Order Form

So I can manage my own career, please send me:
_*Published! Now Sell It!* $14.95

Order books by our authors:

_Guion, Joseph, *Love Songs on the Journey,* $12.95

_Keating, Jean C., *Amorous Accident,* $12.99

_Keating, Jean C., *Pawprints on My Heart,* $19.99

_Keating, Jean C., *Paw Prints Through the Years,*
$28.00

_Roberson, Mildred H.B. and Smith, Claudine Curry, *My Bag Was Always Packed: The Life and Times of a Virginia Midwife.* $14.00

_Sikes, Mary Montague, *Hearts Across Forever,*
$8.95

_Sikes, Mary Montague, *Hotels to Remember,* $45.00

BookWaves
P.O. Box 182
West Point, VA 23181

On-line store
www.BookWaves.net

Notes